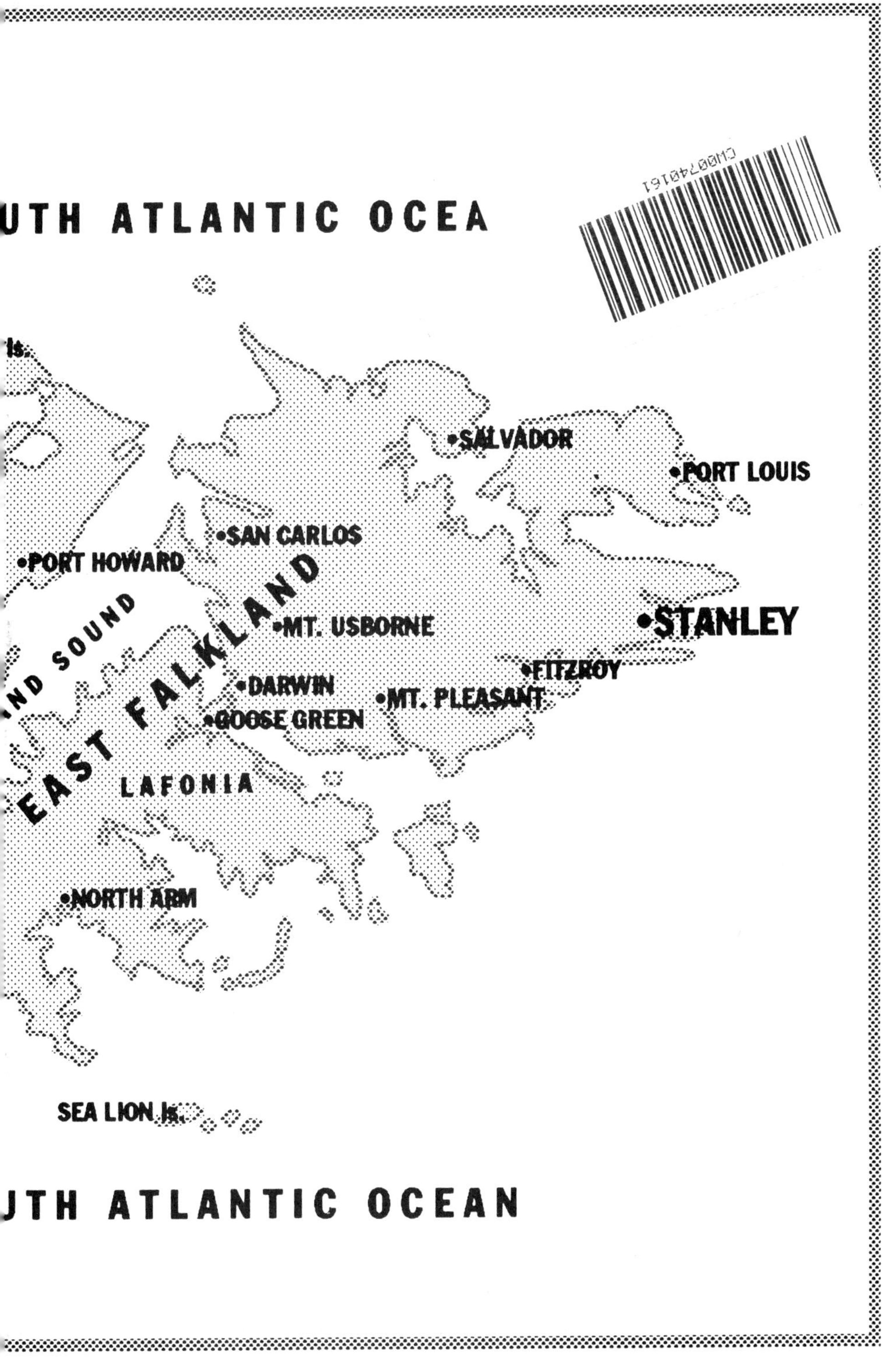

UTH ATLANTIC OCEA
Is.
SALVADOR
PORT LOUIS
SAN CARLOS
PORT HOWARD
EAST FALKLAND
ND SOUND
MT. USBORNE
STANLEY
FITZROY
DARWIN
MT. PLEASANT
GOOSE GREEN
LAFONIA
NORTH ARM
SEA LION Is.
JTH ATLANTIC OCEAN

To Karl with
all my love now
and always xx
        Moira

Falkland People

Angela Wigglesworth

Falkland People

With a Foreword by
Lord Shackleton

 Peter Owen · *London*

PETER OWEN PUBLISHERS
73 Kenway Road London SW5 0RE

First published in Great Britain 1992
© Angela Wigglesworth 1992

A catalogue record for this book is
available from the British Library

ISBN 0-7206-0850-3

Text design by Juliet Standing

*All the photographs are by Norman Clark, with the exception of
the following: pp. 23, 36, 40, 80, 88, 89, 95, 99, 122, 125, 133,
135 and the colour photographs between pp. 70 and 71 (Angela
Wigglesworth); pp. 102, 104, 105 (Steve Howlett); p. 92 (Peter
Gilding); p. 113 (Ann Prior); p. 129 (MOD).*

Printed in Great Britain by Billings of Worcester

Foreword

This book is a painstaking labour of love. But the Falkland Islands are unique in providing the opportunity for such a detailed personal account of the lives and indeed nature of their inhabitants. Angela Wigglesworth has acquired a knowledge and an understanding of the people of the Falklands: both those who were born in the Falklands (known as Kelpers) and those who have emigrated there in recent years.

This is both a social study and a geographical description of the Falkland Islands and their people. It tells a true story of the lives of many people living under demanding conditions in isolated communities, some of which scarcely deserve the name of community, being no more than a solitary farmhouse. It portrays a communal life which until recently was united by radio telephones by which everyone could listen in to everyone else. The thumbnail sketches of the houses in which these people live, the descriptions of the landscape and flowers and especially the interests of the people, set against a background of the long-term threat of Argentine invasion, make this almost compulsory reading for anyone intending to visit the Falklands. For those who do not have that opportunity, it is a winning story.

The Rt Hon. Lord Shackleton, KG, FRS

Acknowledgements

I would like to thank the Falkland Islands Tourist Board for their financial assistance; Les and Peggy Halliday, Roddy and Lilly Napier, and Rob McGill for their generous hospitality to me while I was in the Islands; David Taylor and Eric Ogden for sharing their knowledge of the Falklands with me; Kate Pool of the Society of Authors and Araminta Whitley for their valuable advice; Sukey Cameron, Falkland Islands' Government representative in London, and Robin Lee, Managing Director of Falklands Landholdings Ltd, for reading the MS; Christopher Moore for checking the page proofs. I would also like to thank others who helped me with the book in a variety of practical ways: Jeremy Buck, MRO; Brian McGreal, Falkland Islands Company; Richard Quarrell; Anna King; photographers Tony Tree and David Haskins; Christopher Wigglesworth.

I am greatly indebted to the following people and organisations for their generous donations which made possible the colour photographs in the book: the Rt. Hon. Alan Beith, MP; Norman Black, Chartered Standard Bank, Stanley; Bristow Helicopters Ltd; the Hon. Lucinda Buxton; Air Vice-Marshal David Crwys-Williams; Richard Esdale, Society Expeditions; Mr C. R. Erskine-Hill; Jimmy Forster; John Hamilton; Sir Cosmo Haskard; Keith and Jean Howman; the Rt. Hon. Sir Russell Johnston, MP; Tim Miller, Stanley Growers; Eric Ogden; Robert Patton; Maureen Peapell; Mr P. J. Pepper; Christopher S. Pringle; Dik Sawle; the Scots Guards; Major R. N. Spafford; David Taylor, Governor of Montserrat; the Rt. Hon. Viscount Thurso of Ulster, JP; Major J. A. Valdes-Scott, Sport Elite Ltd; Mr R. O. Venables; Catherine Wigglesworth; the Rt. Hon. Baroness Young, DL.

A.W.

Introduction

I first went to the Falklands in 1986 with a group of journalists to write about the Islands as a holiday destination. It seemed incongruous at the time, just four years after the war, but already wildlife tour companies from Britain were operating there and tourists beginning to trickle in. Our visit coincided with the setting-up of a 150-mile fishing zone, which required fishing vessels from all over the world to buy licences to operate in Falkland waters. My colleagues interviewed politicians and took their stories down to Cable and Wireless for transmission to the UK; others were excited by the wildlife. I was captivated by the Falkland Islanders themselves.

Kelpers, as those who are born there are called (from the thick green seaweed that swirls round the beaches), are friendly and relaxed and speak in an accent you might think came from Devon or New Zealand. They are self-reliant because they have to be – if something needs to be done there's probably only themselves to do it – and they are immensely hospitable. You only have to stop to admire the roses in one of the cottage-garden conservatories, as I did, to be invited in for tea, with scones and diddledee jam made from the tiny berries that grow wild in the grass.

Before the 1982 war with Argentina, few people had heard of the Falklands, let alone knew where they were. A mere dot on the map, they lie deep in the South Atlantic, 8,000 miles from Britain, 300 from the coast of South America and 1,000 from the Antarctic peninsula. Controversy over their sovereignty has raged since they were first sighted in 1592, but one of the few undisputed facts is that the first man to land on them was an Englishman and he did so in 1690.

There are two main islands (East and West Falkland, separated by Falkland Sound) and over 300 smaller ones; they cover an area 160 miles wide, roughly half the size of Wales. Over 2,000 people live here (though this figure is doubled by the 2,000 military personnel still based on the Islands) with around 1,600 in Stanley, the Islands' capital and only town, and others scattered in isolated settlements in Camp. This is the local name for everywhere outside Stanley and comes from the Spanish word 'campo' meaning countryside.

The only way to get to the Falklands from Britain is by Tristar from RAF Brize Norton, a comfortable but no-frills, no-alcohol-on-board, eighteen-hour journey with a brief stop at Ascension Island for refuelling. On arrival at Mount Pleasant Airport on East Falkland there's a lecture, mainly for the military who fill the plane apart from a few holiday-makers, on the dangers of picking up ammunition and straying across wired-off minefields. This is unlikely to be a problem for tourists, but going on a country walk around Stanley does take on a slightly different tone when you are advised to consult the Royal Engineers' minefield map before doing so.

It was December and the Falklands' summer on my first visit, but as we arrived at the then new multi-million-pound airport at Mount Pleasant, there was a sudden violent snowstorm. 'You can have four seasons in any one day,' said an apologetic chaplain there to greet the servicemen, 'but it should get better by tea time.' This was our first taste of the Britishness of the Falklands. Everything stops for tea or 'smoko', the local word for a short break, which includes not only coffee or tea but platefuls of little iced cakes and biscuits.

Bob Stewart, the only civilian bus driver in the Falklands, was waiting at the airport to take us the 35 miles into Stanley along a newly built road with a surface that was considered dangerous enough to merit a 40-mile-an-hour speed limit, although you probably only saw one car every ten minutes. We passed lagoons, a solitary military truck, a solitary Portacabin, road signs denoting the wired-off minefields, and the unique 'stone runs' that are like rivers of white stones coursing down the windswept mountains.

The bird-watchers amongst us already had their binoculars out, for the wildlife of the Falklands is stunning. Penguins breed in their thousands on the rocky shores, elephant seals and sea lions slumber on the beaches, and 185 species of birds have been seen here. We saw some of them in the next few days as we travelled to isolated settlements in the eight-seater Islander planes that provide a taxi service and take off from rough grass once the sheep (there are 650,000 of them in total) have been cleared away. Flying at 500 feet you have the whole empty panorama of the Falklands spread beneath you, with scattered sheep and an occasional solitary farmhouse on the foam-rimmed islands, which look like giant pieces of jigsaw waiting to be pushed together. Cross-country transport is by Land Rover with local drivers who know how to manoeuvre their way along boggy tracks, over grassland and through creeks.

The pictures of barren countryside and freezing conditions that were flashed round the world in those seventy-four days in 1982 have stayed in people's minds as an image of the Falklands. But it's a distorted picture and Islanders are understandably irritated at the interminable references to their supposedly terrible climate. One farmer told me: 'If you spent thirty nights out on the moors in Britain in the middle of winter you might think that was an awful place too.' Richard Hawkins, who sailed up the northern shores of the Falklands in 1594, described the Islands as 'a goodly champion country much of the disposition of England and as temperate', which could be an accurate description of them today. They are the same distance south of the Equator as London is north but have less rain and more wind. Admittedly, they have freak snowstorms any time of the year but on a subsequent visit, the sun shone almost every day for the three weeks I was there, the temperature was in the high seventies and people were sunbathing on the green in front of Stanley's Upland Goose Hotel.

In 1988, two years after the lucrative (for the Falkland Islands' Government) fishing zone had been established and the Islands' annual income had soared from £3 million to £35 million, I had the opportunity to go down again to write about the difference this new-found wealth had made to the Islanders' way of life. Little, I discovered, had changed. There were still no roads outside Stanley, no badly needed new school, no television (but plenty of videos), no telephone except in Stanley. People in Camp still communicated with each other and with the doctor and vet (who held morning surgeries over the air) by the very public radio-telephone system.

The reason no money had been spent on these amenities was that it was extremely difficult to decide what the Islanders' priorities were, and particularly difficult for a government that until 1982 had only been used to dealing with matters any small town council in Britain might have to cope with. Members were often divided over what should come first with the result that nothing came at all. They had niggling worries, too, that the supply of fish might be exhausted by over-fishing, and the lucrative licence money dry up. And how long, some of them wondered, would the British Government be prepared to pay the annual £64 million being spent on the Islands' defence? It was not surprising that they were nervous, for Britain had given no money for development to the Falklands in the 150 years it had owned the Islands, and in the 1970s emigration had increased when it was realised that Britain had been quietly trying to dispose of them to Argentina. But a change in a society that had changed little over the past century was now inevitable and although some Islanders regretted the passing of the old relaxed ways, they also wanted the benefits, like the direct air-link with Britain, of the new.

Many books have now been published about the Falklands War, the Islands' history and the unusual and beautiful wildlife there. But little has been written about the Islanders themselves, about their way of life, their Britishness and their loyalty to Britain even though, surprisingly, they didn't all automatically have British citizenship until December 1982. Hundreds of journalists have visited the Islands since the war but, one woman told me, 'They always talk to politicians and never come to speak to people like us.' I decided to write a book about 'people like us', people from all walks of life, and in the spring of 1990, I returned to the Falklands to work on it.

It was good to be back. Rather like coming home. At Mount Pleasant Airport, Les Halliday, the Customs Officer and Harbour Master, asked me why I'd come. 'To write a book about Falkland Islanders,' I told him. 'Mind you get it right,' he said and I said I'd try.

Bob Stewart in his woolly cap, still the only civilian bus driver, was there to meet the plane and drive us into Stanley. After a short while, he stopped the bus, got off and peered through his binoculars. 'What is he doing in the middle of nowhere?' asked one of the newly arrived passengers. 'This is not nowhere,' replied an Islander. 'This is the main road.'

In fact, Bob had gone to look for people he was to pick up and take to Stanley. They were members of the Falkland Families Association, an organisation formed after the Conflict to enable those who had lost husbands, fathers or sons in it to come down and stay with local families. This had helped them all to come to terms with the situation. 'We want them to know how much we feel for them and the sense of guilt we have that they should have lost loved ones for us,' a farmer's wife told me later. One mother, whose son had been killed on *HMS Sheffield*, admitted she hadn't wanted to come. 'I thought it would be too unsettling,' she said. 'But I'm glad I did. I now know the people he died for and that helps.'

The face of Stanley had changed since my previous visit. Work had started on improving the streets; there was a greater choice of goods on sale in the West Store, the only large shop; and there was nothing unusual (as there would have been before the war) in seeing people of all nationalities in the streets. A new multi-million-pound microwave telephone system had just been installed to enable Islanders outside Stanley to speak to their friends without everyone else listening in, though this is considered a mixed blessing by some who enjoyed the camaraderie of the radio telephone. A new swimming pool had been built; a new school was about to be started; there was a flourishing restaurant and people could see a few hours of television a day, transmitted from the military base at Mount Pleasant. The *Teaberry Express*, a weekly duplicated little newsletter, had joined the more formal fortnightly *Penguin News* to give Islanders gossip about themselves but, as its editor told me, 'Only good news.'

Outside Stanley they were building roads to link isolated settlements, thereby improving the quality of life for those communities where transport had only been possible by plane or horse. There was to be a new ferry to link West and East Falkland. But perhaps the most fundamental change was in the big farm settlements whose owners lived in Britain. Several had been bought by the Falkland Islands' Government and subdivided, with farm workers given the opportunity to buy their own land. This idea – first proposed in the 1976 Shackleton Report – has been generally welcomed, but it does present new social problems. Communities of thirty or forty people are being split up and the new farm owners are moving to their own properties far away from the original settlement; consequently the central shop, social hall and school may be lost because they are no longer economically viable.

It had been left to the old-established and big landowning Falkland Islands Company to provide the kind of sheltered life on a farm that many Islanders still want, and to offer the only training facilities for would-be farmers. Life on an FIC farm has always been comfortably protected: employees get a free house, free peat for cooking and heating that's not only dug for them but delivered to their door, free mutton once a week and free milk. The farm manager, who lives in the Big House, still makes decisions for the shepherds, shearers, handymen, cook and storekeeper employed on the settlement, calling a doctor when necessary, conducting a wedding service, stopping a fight or putting those who drink too much on a blacklist which prevents them buying alcohol for several months and sometimes longer. Employees often don't handle money – they buy things at the local store by signing a chit and the amount is deducted from their salary.

Most of the military personnel in the Falklands come down on a four-month posting, and both they and the Islanders wish that the military base had not been built so far from Stanley. Thirty-five miles on a badly surfaced and dangerous road is a long way to go for a drink in a pub of an evening, and so the men are stuck in their isolated environment. But they're encouraged by the military authorities to go into the countryside in their free time and stay with farming families, who enjoy showing them what the Islands have to offer. Those who do so often grow to love the place and ask to come down for another four months' term of duty.

Day-to-day life for those who live in the Falklands in the 1990s is altering significantly and one or two people have already changed jobs since I met them. But even now, little is known about the Islanders for whom men gave their lives in 1982. I hope this book will rectify that and give a better understanding of these mainly British people, 8,000 miles from Britain, who just want to remain British.

Postscript
The Falkland Islands Company have now sold most of their agricultural land to the Falkland Islands' Government, who assured employees that their employment would be continued and their way of life remain the same.

Angela Wigglesworth
1991

A Short History

1592   Captain John Davis discovers the Islands in his ship the *Desire*.

1594   Islands sighted by Sir Richard Hawkins, who calls them Hawkins Maiden Land.

1598   Islands sighted by Dutch navigator Sebald de Weert.

1690   Captain John Strong in his ship the *Welfare* is indisputably the first man to land on the Islands.

1701   The French navigator Gouin de Beauchene lands.

1763   The French name the Islands Iles Malouines after St Malo, the port from which their expedition set out.

1764   The French establish the Port Louis settlement.

1765   John Byron, sent by the British Government to survey the Islands, sets up Port Egmont settlement and claims the Islands for King George III.

1766/7   France hands over the Iles Malouines to Spain. Port Louis is renamed Port Soledad.

1769   Small British force on the Islands confronted by Spanish at Port Egmont and surrenders the settlement.

1770   British leave the Islands.

1771   War is avoided and the British take over Port Egmont again.

1774   Britain evacuates Port Egmont.

1806   Spanish leave settlement at Port Soledad and the Islands are abandoned by everyone except whalers and sealers.

1810   South American colonies are separated from Spain.

1816   The new United Provinces of Rio de la Plata claim the Falklands.

1820   The Governor of the United Provinces takes possession.

1823   First Argentine Governor of Islas Malvinas appointed. Land and fishing rights are given to a Frenchman, Louis Vernet.

1828   Louis Vernet is appointed Governor of the Islands.

1831   The Americans sack Louis Vernet's settlement as a reprisal for the seizing of American sealers, and declare Islands free of all governance.

1832   Spanish Governor takes over Port Louis (Soledad).

1833   Britain returns to the Falklands and begins to colonise them. March: Charles Darwin visits the Islands on the *Beagle*.

1840   The Colonial Lands and Emigration Commissioners propose colonising the Islands.

1841   Richard Moody is appointed Governor of the Islands.

1845   Stanley becomes the new capital and seat of government.

1851	Falkland Islands Company is formed.
1869	All of West Falkland leased for farming.
1892	Britain makes the Falklands a crown colony.
1914	Battle of the Falkland Islands, in which the British naval squadron defeats German squadron.
1939	Stanley becomes a radio base and telegraphy station in World War II.
1964	A Condor group from Argentina 'invades' the Falklands. Islanders tell United Nations Committee on Decolonisation that they want to retain links with Britain.
1968	Four unofficial members of the Islands Council appeal to British MPs to prevent the Government making an agreement with Argentina. Lord Chalfont visits the Falklands to discuss their future.
1971	Communications Agreement signed between Britain and Argentina, and first direct communications link established between them. Shipping link with Montevideo, Uruguay stops.
1972	Argentina builds temporary airstrip at Stanley.
1976	Lord Shackleton's *Economic Survey of the Falkland Islands* is published.
1977	British-built airport opens at Cape Pembroke. Britain and Argentina discuss sovereignty.
1980	The Hon. Nicholas Ridley MP, Minister of State at the Foreign Office, comes to the Falklands and discusses how the sovereignty dispute could be resolved.
1981	Talks on the subject at the UN. The Islands' legislature calls for a freeze in negotiations.
1982	April 2: Argentine forces invade the Falklands. May 1: British Task Force moves into Exclusion Zone. May 21: British Task Force lands at San Carlos, East Falkland. June 14: Commander of Argentine forces surrenders. September: Lord Shackleton's 1976 report is updated. British Government announce a grant of £31 million in aid to implement the report's development plan.
1983	January: Margaret Thatcher visits the Falklands.
1985	May 12: New airport at Mount Pleasant officially opened by HRH Prince Andrew.
1986	November: Britain declares 150-mile Interim Fisheries Conservation and Management Zone round the Islands.
1990	February: Diplomatic relations are resumed between Britain and the Argentine. April: Britain lifts the 150-mile protection zone around the Falklands. October: Duke of Kent visits the Falklands. December: Falklands Outer Conservation Zone declared for fisheries conservation.
1991	March: HRH the Duke of Edinburgh visits the Falklands.

Stanley

Stanley, on the east coast of East Falkland, became the capital of the Falklands in 1845 and was named after Lord Stanley, the Secretary of State for the Colonies. Today, with a population of 1,600, it is the Falklands' only town.

Houses with brightly painted roofs are clustered along the seashore and spread in straight lines up the side of a hill. There are potted plants in their conservatories, and the gardens behind white fences and fuchsia hedges are full of poppies, lupins, roses and pinks. Adjoining most of the houses are covered stacks of peat, used for cooking and heating, though some families have changed to diesel oil.

The West Store is the largest shop in town and sells just about everything. There are around twenty-five other small shops, four pubs, eleven hotels and guest houses, three churches including a cathedral, and a town hall that has a post office, philatelic bureau, magistrates' court, library and dance hall within it. In addition, Stanley has a hospital, two schools, a hostel for children from Camp [see p. 9] to stay in during term time, a museum, golf course, police station with honeysuckle growing up the wall, a swimming pool, three restaurants and a bomb-disposal unit. Government House stands on the edge of the town and ships battered from trips around Cape Horn in the last century lie wrecked in the harbour.

The Company Director

*Dik Sawle, former expat
teacher, is now director of a
fishing company; he is
married to Judith and they
have a young son.*

You sign on blind in the UK to come here and don't realise you're going to be doing the same kind of job as a local person but getting three times the pay and preferential treatment. You come in for quite a lot of criticism because of that.

The day I made it in the Falklands was when I ditched a Spanish lesson with Class 4B and put a rear cab on the back of a Land Rover. They were impressed that an expat could do that. You have to get your hands oily here and if you don't, you don't enter into Falklands life.

The Bus Driver

Bob Stewart, 51, came from Inverness in 1958 to work on a farm settlement and now runs the only civilian bus service on the Islands. He is married to his second wife, Celia, and has four children from a former marriage.

I didn't even know where the Falklands were when I applied for the contract in 1958, and I hadn't farmed before – I'd worked on the railways – so it was a new experience. At that time, you had to ride everywhere on horseback and ask the farm manager if you could borrow a horse, unless you were a shepherd and had your own. Even in Stanley there were very few vehicles.

After two and a half years I found I wasn't suited to farm life, broke my contract and started working for the Government, first as a labourer then a plumber. When they decided that the new airport was not going to be built near Stanley [it is 35 miles away] I thought there would be a need for a bus service and approached the Falkland Islands Development Corporation to see if they would help me get one going. I got a loan but can't reveal the figure because that was part of the agreement.

The airport road then was better than it is now. In fact, it's deteriorated a lot and is very dangerous. I've had punctures and breakdowns and seen many accidents, though mostly with visitors and not local people. On average I keep to the 40 mph speed limit, though when I'm on my own I go slightly faster. But I don't take that road for granted.

I now have three 52-seater coaches and two 12-seater minibuses, and go to Mount Pleasant to meet the Tristar for incoming and outgoing passengers. I try to give the best personal service I can and everyone is taken to or from their own doorsteps. On Tuesdays and Fridays I take the vegetables from the hydroponic nursery in Stanley to Mount Pleasant and pick up the air cargo, which could be anything from small computers and personal baggage to ships' spares.

In the summer I have the cruise ships coming in, and take tourists round Stanley or to Goose Green and Fitzroy. People are always keenly interested in what Falkland life has got to offer and to hear about the Conflict. I tell them the good and the bad things. I said to some of the Falkland Families [see p. 13] who were down here recently, 'Although it's a very, very sad occasion that you're down here, I feel I must elaborate on the point that it's nice to have you because the British public believed we weren't worth fighting for.'

What I try to put over is that we are almost all British

people or descendants from them and talk the Queen's English. We have a few foreign nationals but probably less than 2%. I told some of the families: 'If you go back and look at the previous world wars, young people left the Falklands and died for an ideal of the British public. It was a cause. The Falklands supplied aircraft, six Spitfires, I believe. I mean, surely that ideal should still be alive today in this generation?'

The Assistant Radio Producer

Wendy Teggart, 39, is the third eldest of nine children and has six of her own. Born in Stanley, she married an Englishman and went to live in England for four years. Divorced in 1983, she has now remarried, lives in Stanley and works at FIBS, the Falkland Islands Broadcasting Station. Her granddaughter, aged 5, is probably the first eighth-generation Islander in the Falklands.

I love working with radio — I don't think of it as being work and would probably do it for nothing. Patrick Watts is the Station Manager and there are three of us full-time and six part-time. We have five continuity announcers, who come in and read the news. They all have other jobs but come in just because they like working here.

It's a friendly service and I wouldn't like to think it was ever going to change that much. One announcer, when she was reading the news the other night, had to admit, 'I'm really sorry but I can't read my own writing' — and I'd hate it if we ever lost that informality. I said to Patrick when he first gave me the job, 'I can't do it like the BBC and if I say something wrong I'm not going to say "I do apologise".' 'What are you going to say?' he asked. I told him, 'Probably whatever comes into my head.' In fact, the first time I did make a mistake I said 'Oh God' and people were laughing because no one had ever said anything like that before.

We cover about six hours of the twenty-four the station is on the air, starting at ten o'clock in the morning and going through to 12.30 pm, when we hand over to BFBS [British Forces Broadcasting Service at Mount Pleasant]. We come back at 5.30 in the afternoon and go through to 9.30 pm each day except Friday when we go on to 10.30 pm.

A lot of it is BBC transcriptions, locally produced record programmes, and the Falklands in *World News*. Our *News Magazine* programme covers the courts, births, marriages and deaths, people visiting the Islands, and public events, in fact everything that happens here. The radio is our equivalent to a daily newspaper, which we don't have. The flight times of the Islander planes, with the names of the people travelling in them, go out three times a day, so those booked to fly the following day can hear what time they'll be picked up or dropped off, or whether in fact they're going to fly that day at all, because sometimes there are too many bookings and they have to wait until the next day. Three evenings a week, people can advertise what they have for sale for 10p a word.

We put out emergency announcements, anything from missing children to house fires. It doesn't happen very often but just occasionally we'll get a little one who's wandered off. Of course, the Falklands being the friendly, open place it is, you don't really worry for an hour or so, but after a while you might get a little bit anxious and the quickest way to find someone is to put a message over the radio and ask if anyone has seen them and if so, to phone in.

There was a time that, when our fire sirens went off, we would automatically, no matter what time of day or night, come down here and broadcast where the fire was. Now the Fire Department has a bleeper system, so it would only be in the event of a really bad one when they needed more volunteers to help that we'd come down and broadcast.

The Fish and Chip Shop Owners

Pauline and Dave Hawksworth came from Barnsley, Yorkshire in 1983 to run the Woodbine Café and fish and chip shop takeaway in Stanley. They have three children.

PAULINE, 40: We had a fish and chip shop in Barnsley and the thing that first got us interested in the Falklands was when we saw a TV programme about them and heard what the people needed out here.

Dave came down for a month to have a look around and got the option on buying a house. We thought about it for three weeks and then decided to come. It took about six months to settle everything and I was a bit apprehensive because I'd only seen photographs.

In actual fact it was better than I thought because Dave had purposely painted things a bit blacker than they really were. We brought everything with us, including an electric frying range because a peat stove wouldn't have been consistent enough.

We opened in January 1984 and as they hadn't had a fish and chip shop before, it was rather slow to start with. I think most people thought we'd be here for six months and then pack it in, because there have been so many ventures when people have started something and then given up. We did have a bit of difficulty getting people to try our mushy peas, which is something everyone in Yorkshire has. No one would try them at first but now they're one of our best-selling things.

We have a big walk-in freezer and get fish supplies when we can. Sometimes a local person goes fishing, but we can't rely on that. We use a ton of potatoes a month direct from the ships and make our own pies, burgers, sausage and bread rolls. We can seat thirty-two people in the café, and it's now going very well. On Saturdays we usually do about 300 lunches.

It's hard work in one sense but very rewarding, and I think if we weren't doing what people wanted us to, there's no way they'd patronise us. They appreciate anyone here who does something and sticks to it, and they understand if we just want to close for a week and go off somewhere. There's Sports Week coming up at the end of February so we'll go off to Hill Cove on West Falkland for that.

We've now bought three 50-acre plots at Fitzroy, where we relax and fish in the river, and also a little island of about 2,000 acres off West Falkland, where we go whenever we get the chance. We bought that for £10,000 and it's a lovely place with elephant seals, penguins and peregrine falcons and a very basic little house. It's mainly a tussac [long grass that grows to a height of 10 feet from a thick raised base] island, but that's been eaten out by the sheep, and we've been doing some fencing to let it grow again. We have a few sheep there now and someone has shown us how to shear them and roll the wool and press it.

The children love it here. Jeanette is going to Peter Symonds' College in the UK to take A levels, and Chris just likes everything about the Falklands, particularly going out to Camp and helping with the horses and shearing.

DAVE, 43: The thing I used to miss out here at first was fresh milk – there wasn't any until two years ago when the dairy was started – it was all UHT and powdered milk. The fresh-fruit situation has eased a lot too since we began getting the *Indiana* from Chile. Before that we were buying and selling fresh fruit from South Africa on a monthly basis – people just went mad for it and no one ever asked the price. We'd get through about £1,500 worth of stuff in two hours.

Coming to the Falklands was a case of if we failed we failed, and if we survived we survived, but as long as we stayed together that was the main thing. We've been married twenty years this April but going off doing something like this that's a bit mad can often split families, can't it?

The Governor

Before coming to the Falklands, William Fullerton worked for Shell International Petroleum in Uganda, in the British Embassy in Pakistan, as Ambassador to Somalia in Mogadishu, and in the Ministry of Defence as an Arabist on defence export services.

My job in the Falklands is very different from being an ambassador – it's much more varied and interesting and one gets involved in far more things. One of the issues facing the Falklands today is oil exploration, though we don't yet know if there is any, as no real in-depth surveys have been done. I think the Falkland Islands' Government is not going to say there can't be any exploration, but I think we do have to get our legislation tied up first. There are some Islanders who are interested in it but I think there is an anxiety and it's a legitimate worry. Part of the joy of being in the Falklands is because they are as they are now, with the peace and quiet and special quality of life. A lot of oil companies stamping round the place would certainly change that. I know some Councillors went to the Shetlands and were fairly impressed with the way the oil had been managed in that it didn't ruin the lifestyle of the people, but I haven't been myself so don't know what it's like.

There are a lot of advantages working in a small community. People come here to Government House with their problems, and ask me about housing or whatever, and I'm very happy for them to do so. Obviously I don't rush round undercutting officials – I don't have that kind of power – but I do listen to what they have to say and sometimes one can get attention focused on something that has slipped through. I like to do that.

I also like the do-it-yourself society. When I first came and saw that my paddock out there was knee-deep in grass, I rang up the Public Works Department and said, 'What about whoever mows it coming to mow it?' but there wasn't anyone, nor anything to mow it with, which is why we now have nine sheep! That's fun and I enjoy having them. We're just marking the lambs and we've shorn four of them – not me personally yet, but I will learn to – and we sold a fleece, so that's a bit of money for the cathedral. The same do-it-yourself attitude had to apply to the fences too. There aren't enough people to paint them so I've done a lot myself, which I find quite therapeutic. I like the fact that you don't just hang around saying 'Who do I ring up to do it?' – you get on and have a go.

I think everyone would like to see more of the servicemen come into Stanley but it's quite an effort to drive 35 miles to have dinner and then go back again. They do come for sports occasions and also do valuable voluntary work here. Anyone who really wants to be friendly with local people doesn't find it difficult, but for someone who's a bit shy it's quite hard to know how to begin.

I think everyone is hopeful that Britain and Argentina will resume normal relations, but the Islanders simply don't want anything to do with Argentina themselves. You can see the reason why. If you're used to a British way of life, have British law and everything else British in your lifestyle, what would you feel if someone invited you to transfer yourself lock, stock and barrel to some totally foreign country where they spoke a different language, had different customs, different economy and not a very cheerful one at that?

The Radio-Telephone Operator

Eileen Videl, 64, is married and has had twelve children, three of whom died.

I started working the radio telephone about nine years ago. I needed a job and just went into the exchange. They said, 'There's the microphone, have a go.'

Before the new telephone system came in at the end of 1989, people had the radio telephone as the link from Camp to Stanley, and the doctors had a half-hour morning surgery on it. That was quite difficult for people. It was all right if they just had a cold but if you had something a bit more wrong with you it wasn't very good to have to talk about it over the radio. If I couldn't get someone at their home, I'd find them in all sorts of places. For instance, if the person was a farmer, there was a good chance he was going to the bank or the West Store and I'd make contact with him there.

I remember the day of the Argentine invasion. You weren't meant to be out on the streets but they asked me if I would try and get all the kids from Camp who were at school in Stanley and put them in touch with their parents. An [Argentine] officer came and fetched me with one of the schoolteachers, and we went along with all these kids and each of them spoke to their mums and said they were OK. The Argentines were always very polite – there were no cases of assault or anything. Letting the children make these phone calls to their parents on the first morning was quite a thoughtful thing to do, especially as the young officer who drove me had had his best friend killed at Government House that morning.

When the children had sent their messages, I was just going home when I suddenly heard, 'Hello, Stanley, this is *Endurance*' [the Royal Navy patrol ship in the Antarctic] over the radio. They asked if I could tell them what the situation was in Stanley. It was risky because you didn't know who was listening in, but I told them that on Davis Street where I lived, troops had passed us coming in and we reckoned about 5,000 had arrived that first day. I also told him about the armed troop carriers and the type of aircraft they had and the ships and helicopters here. Then the voice said, 'Hold on a minute,' and whoever it was went away and got the captain and I had to tell him everything all over again. I might have got away with it once, twice was asking for trouble. Anyway I told him and said, 'For God's sake, stay the hell out of it.' I had visions of *Endurance* coming in and taking on the whole Argentine fleet. You could see the big ships outside, and the helicopters were buzzing all round the camp. The *Endurance* passed the message on to London about what it was like in Stanley, and it was the first word they'd had out after the invasion, which was only a matter of hours.

A few days after that I was watching one of the Argentine transport ships taking on all the landing craft. We weren't sure where they were going that night but I got up early next morning and watched them go off, heading in the general direction of Darwin. When I got to work I called up Darwin and said, 'I think you're going to have some visitors about lunch time.' Brook Hardcastle, the farm manager, called me up before lunch to say 'the visitors' had just anchored. But he did have that little bit of warning.

The first time I spoke to the British navy was about a week before the surrender. A voice suddenly came over the radio: 'This is the British navy' – it was during the doctors' session!

At one point there were only about a hundred people left in Stanley, most had gone out to Camp, but I didn't want to go. I was here when they invaded and thought I'd stay to the end.

The Doctor

Dr Robin McIlroy, 68, worked in the UK, Saudi Arabia and Australia before coming to the Falklands in 1985. His wife is a magistrate and they have two daughters.

There are four civilian and two military doctors in Stanley, and two up at Mount Pleasant. On an average day I set off from home about eight o'clock in the morning and apart from when I'm on call, which is one day in four, I generally finish by about five o'clock in the afternoon.

With the distances we have to cover going out to Camp or on the ships, it's almost impossible for one doctor to do one job, so we share them all. We try and get round the bigger settlements at least once in six weeks and the smaller ones every twelve weeks, staying in one house where those who are well enough come and see us, and we trot round to see the others who aren't.

A lot of little problems pile up in a three-month period and we find very nearly everyone comes to see us. Perhaps they just come for a talk – it's quite a social occasion. In fact, having time to talk is the biggest difference between being in practice here and in the UK. It was one of the reasons I left Britain. I had about 3,000 patients to look after and you certainly didn't have time to sit and talk then. Here we have time for individual patients, though when the fishing fleets are in and you find fourteen Koreans sitting on your doorstep, things get a bit hectic. Seventy-five per cent of all illnesses would probably get better anyway eventually, and most of what we do is to make patients a bit more comfortable while their own bodies get them better. The sort of illness is remarkably constant all over the world: coughs and colds, ladies who complain their husbands don't pay them enough attention, and ladies who complain their husbands pay them too much attention. Life is a bit more peaceful here, a bit slower, but there are still lingering stresses from the Conflict. I'm just finding that those who lived through it are only now beginning to talk to me about it. Few people were killed but nearly all of them lived under occupation conditions with foreign soldiers marching up and down outside the houses. There is a very real fear it could happen again.

Because the population in Camp is so small, not more than 500 or 600 people, you get to know them quite well and the sort of problems they usually have, and it's surprising what you could get across by gently hinting at things when we had to talk on the radio telephone. Some wrote to us, and the telephone will make a tremendous difference to the ladies who don't want their gynae-cological problems broadcast over the air. In fact, a lot of people got to know what to do about their own problems by listening to other people's, and another thing we often tend to forget is that, because everyone heard what was going on, if Mrs X was ill, her neighbours went round to see what they could do for her. With the new telephone system, Mrs X will have to ring her neighbours herself to ask for help.

Our aircraft are not equipped for night flying and we don't have landing lights at the [Stanley] airfield but very occasionally in an emergency Islander planes have flown at night with two Land Rovers shining their lights at each end of the runway. For real night emergencies we call on the army helicopter service and they help us out. We have a surgeon and anaesthetist but it would be ridiculously expensive to have a body-scanning machine down here costing a quarter of a million pounds, which might be used only three times a year. Our biggest worry is what to do with a very small premature or sick baby, because it's impossible to have all the equipment or expertise to deal with this. If we can see there might be trouble, we try to persuade the mother to go to England. But some people would rather take the risk and stay here and that's their decision. Before the war, all the complicated cases went either to Uruguay or the British Hospital in Buenos Aires.

There is no formal structure of social services here, no government sickness pay scheme except for people who work for the Government or big companies. We do have a welfare scheme but it's on an individual one-off basis. Our Welfare Officer, who is on the hospital staff and a fifth-generation Falkland Islander, knows just about everything about everybody and is an enormous help. If anyone is short in any way, their situation is assessed by the Medical Department on how much rent they have to pay, whether they're by themselves, in a house with a big fire or electric stove. We try to bring the income up to roughly the level of a government old-age pension of around £40 a week and get those who we know are complete spendthrifts to bring their grocery and electricity bills for us to pay, to make sure the money doesn't all go into the pub. If anyone feels aggrieved, they can appeal to their Councillor, who will bring it up at various government committees.

The Hospital Matron

Mandy Heathman worked at Westminster Hospital, London, before coming down to the Falklands on a six-month contract in 1985. She is now married to Keith, a contract shearer. The King Edward VII Memorial Hospital, Stanley, has thirty-two beds, with twenty civilian and six military staff, and takes civilian and military patients.

Before I came, I met someone at the Falkland Islands' Government office in London and he told me what life was like down here. He said you knitted and read of an evening and I'd need a long dress to go out in. In fact, I've only worn a long dress once and that was to my wedding, and I've never done any knitting. But the do's and don'ts are quite formal at times and you can wear a long dress to dances.

If people require specialist medical treatment they have to go to the UK, and if there's likely to be a difficult pregnancy they have to go at thirty-five weeks and are not allowed back until four weeks after the birth. In the UK you tend to have different wards for different specialities. Down here we've just got one hospital so you get an enormous variety of things. The fishing season brings in tremendous injuries and you deal with them the best you can. People on the boats get very tired – they have to fish all night in the jigger waiting for the squid to come into the light, and then they have to pack it all before getting any sleep. The squid hooks are horrible little things, with fifteen or twenty hooks on each one, and the men catch them in their fingers. But the money they make every day is an enormous sum and it's not worth their while stopping jigging to come in with injuries. If anyone is very badly hurt they call a helicopter but otherwise they just wait until they get back, by which time they've usually got to lose a finger because the infection is so bad. We have men from Japan, Korea, Taiwan, and quite a few from the Eastern-bloc countries.

People from Europe can usually speak a bit of English or Spanish, and the Chief Medical Officer's wife is Polish, so she can communicate with the Russians. Once they've got over their initial fear of coming into hospital we don't need an interpreter for the day-to-day things, you just do actions and can have a hilarious time trying to demonstrate 'Could you wee in this bottle?' Different nurses go on the district with the doctor each month and people living there save things up until then.

There's a big alcohol problem here and most accidents are usually related to it. There's very little to do and alcohol is cheap. Winter is the worst because it gets dark early, so you finish work, go to the pub for a quick drink and then stay there for the rest of the evening.

It's not easy for women to go into pubs, although it's better than it was, but when Keith and I go out together I'm considered fairly weird to go into one. In fact they are not really pubs, more like bars. We always go to dances when they have them, probably about once a month, but the May Ball is the big event when people vote for the prettiest girl for the May Queen. The girls have dresses brought down from the UK, do their hair up with flowers, wear big sashes and look absolutely beautiful. They have to dance round and their fathers dance with them and give everyone else real frosty looks!

They also have these things called two-nighters, which is a dance, steer riding and a big booze-up all over one weekend. They need a nurse there in case anyone falls off a steer, though this doesn't normally do much damage because the men are fairly drunk so quite relaxed when they fall.

We live in so-called Sin City in Eliza Cove near the road to the airport and it takes about a quarter of an hour to walk to the hospital. It got its name because everyone who used to live here was living in sin, but now they're all married so we've lost our reputation. The house is two Wyseman-plan [prefabricated] buildings that we got from Mount Pleasant – a cabin costs about £4,500. We cut our own peat, dry it and bring it into Stanley in the tractor. It's free but you have to put a certain amount of time into it and if you haven't got that, you have to pay others to do it. We need about 150 cubic yards, which would take about three days to cut by hand, but with a machine, about one. Giving people in Stanley time to cut their peat of an evening was apparently the reason why the time here is an hour different to Camp time.

The Attorney General

David Lang worked in Nauru, a remote island in the central Pacific, and in the West Indies before coming to the Falklands. He is married with four children and has a house in Somerset.

From the legal point of view, the Falklands were neglected for a long period of time until 1983. They had to do without lawyers and a huge mass of legislation has had to be done in a fairly short period to meet the modern needs of the Islands. This doesn't mean copying UK legislation. One has to look at the size of population, the Islanders' attitudes and ways of life, and try to devise something which is satisfactory to them.

It's difficult for an Attorney General to live in a small community because it's like being in a goldfish bowl and you can't easily let your hair down. I could go for a drink in a pub but the difficulty is that it wouldn't be for relaxation because people would approach me with their problems or with their point of view about something. It's a feature you can either welcome or abhor but it certainly does create a strain.

The legal set-up in the Islands is rather like the UK in miniature. Starting from the bottom, we have a summary court which consists of Justices of the Peace; a magistrates' court which has the same sort of jurisdiction as an English crown court on the criminal side, and jurisdiction on the civil side equivalent to a county court. Above that is the Supreme Court which acts as a court of appeal from the lower courts and also in criminal matters; then there is the Court of Appeal and the Privy Council. So we have a very intricate court system which is basically identical in complication to that of the UK.

We've had no murders here that I know of. There has been a manslaughter, but not in my time, and a couple of rape cases. I bewail the passing of the village bobby in England just as much as the people here question the higher profile of the police. But I think they have to bear in mind that the level and seriousness of crimes committed have very much increased. I attribute this to the rapid pace of change since 1982 which was bound to bring some problems with it. The Islands had a very unstressed existence before then, it was a very peaceful society that could have almost been un-policed, and the economic development has certainly brought stress.

The community is far more competitive now, with more opportunities, and some of the younger people are bound to feel left behind because they can't compete academically. The price of houses has gone up, there are all sorts of social strains and the Islands are far closer to the UK of the eighties and nineties than they were before 1982, when they would probably have equated in many senses with the UK of the 1920s and 1930s. It's sad but one can't halt development which by and large Falkland Islands people welcome. Many Islanders have nostalgia for the old days and would ideally like to have the benefits of the present time without any of the disadvantages. And so would I, by golly, but I have to recognise it's impossible.

The Shopkeeper

Sandra Hirtle, 48, lives in a white weatherboarded and red tin-roofed house in Eliza Cove Road that was originally built as an office for the British Antarctic Survey. At 14, she became a maid in Stanley Hospital, and she was a maid at Goose Green, Hill Cove and Chartres before going back to the hospital at 15 as a probation nurse. In 1985 she began work at the Stanley bakery, and she now runs a grocer's shop.

I first ran the Stanley bakery in 1985 when the owners went away for a while. Then they said they couldn't afford to keep me on, so rather than have the business close, I took it over myself in 1986. It was in an old garage just below where it is now.

It varied what we had to produce. On Mondays and Wednesdays, it was 250 loaves for one order – that's for the Falkland Islands Company – and we had to make bread for our own shop as well. On a Friday we did about 400 to 500 loaves – bloomers, French sticks, bread rolls, baps, cottage loaves, whatever there was time for.

To be honest, I hated baking. I'd rather dig a post hole, put a fence up or strip a house down and rebuild it, than bake. But the baby was put in my lap and I was left holding it. I could have got someone else to work there but we just hadn't got the room.

Towards the end I didn't do a lot of baking myself but I did go down and serve in the shop. The first time an Englishwoman came in and asked me for sliced bread I turned round and said, 'If you're too lazy to slice it you're too lazy to chew it.' I never thought I'd end up with a bread slicer myself. In fact, I didn't think it would catch on with the Islanders, but it has.

I don't eat much bread myself and just have one meal a day in the evening, but as long as it's mutton and potatoes, particularly mutton, I'm all right. I like fish but you can't get it. I used to love going away fishing but now the beaches are out of bounds because of the mines.

There have been so many changes since the Conflict and everyone in Britain goes on about all the money we have and that we should have fur coats and Rolls-Royces. But half the money that comes into the Islands is wasted and it's definitely not going on the locals. If it was, we could be driving on roads that were made of gold and not the stone runs we've got.

But even though the Islands will never be half as good as they used to be, for me, they're God's chosen country. They're still paradise and it's still the only country where you know your children are safe.

The Vet

Peter Armitage was born in Scotland and came with his wife Kay to the Falklands in 1987 after working in New Zealand for four years. They now have a young son, Cameron.

PETER: I get a constant stream of cats to treat but not many dogs because of hydatid, a disease dogs pick up from sheep in the form of parasites which they can transmit to humans. It can kill people very easily and children are particularly at risk: they rub their hands over a dog and put them straight in their mouths.

Every dog in Stanley – I think there are just over sixty including guard dogs down at MPA [Mount Pleasant Airport] – is licensed and, by law, dosed against hydatid every six weeks. The Islanders are so aware of the disease – many know people who have been infected – that a dog is not an acceptable pet and most wouldn't have one in the house. If you look at the ownership of dogs in Stanley, there are only about four or five Falkland Islanders who have them as pets, and most of these are people who've worked with them and don't want to dispose of them. The working collies on farms aren't licensed but they're kept tethered or in kennels.

Many Islanders are very keen on their horses – they were the main working animals on farms until shepherds started using motorbikes. If you walk round Stanley you'll see a lot of horses providing a mobile lawn-mowing service! The gardens are small but can give grazing for a day.

My work is very seasonal – at the moment I'm trying to do a blood test on every ram on the Islands for *brusella ovis*, a disease that affects rams in particular and makes them infertile. There's no treatment for it and if a ram is positive, it's destroyed. It's a venereal disease, sexually transmitted, but an infected ram won't lose his interest in sex and will infect the ewe without getting her pregnant. It's a condition that was first recognised in Australia and New Zealand – but not yet in Britain – and it seems that an imported animal brought the disease into the Falklands. But we've got most farms clean of it now.

One of the few disadvantages for me as a solo vet is that professional contact is very limited and I think I need to be around other vets occasionally to jog my memory and keep me up to date, though I read what I can. Likewise, I've got my particular interests and I'll take the Islands in a certain direction. But I think it could be dangerous if I was down here on my own for too long: other areas could get neglected or there might be things that could be done better or in a different way. Having a change of vets is beneficial, though it can be unsettling for the Islanders.

KAY: I love living in the Falklands. Everyone is so friendly and we have a wonderful social life. At present, two of my good friends have children the same age as Cameron and there's a Jelly Tots Club for the under-fives. If I have an appointment or have to do some shopping, it acts as a crèche.

A lot has changed since we've been here. For one thing, you have more choice in the shops, though you accept that there are certain things you're not going to get, like yoghurt, and you just make it yourself. I suppose what I really miss is the family but the new phone system is wonderful though a bit expensive, as we found out when we got our first bill. But it's just the convenience of being able to pick up the phone, dial and talk. Before, you had either to accept the fact that if you phoned from home the line wasn't going to be very good, or make the journey down to the Cable and Wireless office, which is not far away but it's not the same as chatting in your own home.

The Bank Manager

Norman Black came from Scotland in 1989 as Manager of the Standard Chartered Bank, the first bank in the Falklands.

One of my first tasks was to extend the commercial services to the public and provide more loans for Islanders by way of mortgages, not just for residential houses but commercial and farming purposes too. And to combine that with a partnership agreement with the Falkland Islands Development Corporation so that more ventures could get off the ground.

The movement seven years ago from a government savings bank into a commercial banking venture has been difficult for people. They weren't used to it and we were asking them to understand something that was totally new. I'm often asked: 'I'd like to borrow £5,000 or £1,000 but I don't know how I'm going to repay it.' The initial reaction from a high-street bank in the UK would be to tell them to go somewhere else, but here we ask for further information and say we'll look at it again. I think there's a growing understanding now that we're trying to be helpful not obstructive. It's a question of understanding what they're doing, as much as just looking at figures.

The bank's role here is a bit different from the UK in that we're not just a bank, but the national giro and a consultant business too. It's important that people come to us for assistance and I probably spend 60% of my time giving advice which may not be productive. Someone might come in and say, 'I'm thinking about leaving my husband, what happens to my money?' or, 'I want to buy a house, how do I go about it?' or, 'I want to build an office block, I've got the plans, what do I do now?' You're never quite sure what's going to happen from day to day. I sometimes have to call my colleagues in London for assistance because I can't know everything.

We have 2,200 customers and I think there is a growing use of the bank. It's a close community, the people are very warm, a little bit reticent and shy, but once you get to know them they're very helpful, considerate and extremely honest. The bank has been here seven years now and I don't think we've had one debt caused by an Islander. That must be a record second to none in the world.

The Headmaster

David Burgess taught in Thame, Oxfordshire and in Katmandu and El Salvador before becoming Headmaster of Stanley Secondary School in 1988.

There are 150 children and because this is such a small number we relate very much to the community. Parents and employers come in, the church uses our facilities and we have assembly on Mondays in the cathedral.

You have to have a C-grade GCSE to go to Peter Symonds' College in Winchester, and children are chosen solely on academic grounds, not from the college's choice but the Government's policy. Seven went last year and we have ten there now but I'd like more to go. A worrying feature is that of these ten children who want to do A levels, eight are girls, who are more likely to stay in England because they'll meet men who don't want to come here. I think Falkland Islands boys find it more difficult to cope in the UK because the culture here is very macho, very tough and rural. They may wish to take up executive positions but they're more interested in physical work. The only man in the bank in Stanley is the expatriate manager, because he can't get men to accept that type of work.

When girls do get qualified and come back, they will have infinitely more qualifications than the men and what implication does that have for the future leadership of the Islands? If women are dominant in the higher posts, there'll certainly be a very different flavour to it.

The war did disrupt the flow of education here and we're only now getting back on our feet and making it a proper school again. The children are very traditionalist and want badges to indicate rank of prefect. Some are still scarred by the war and, though they were very young when it happened, they write about violence in a way you wouldn't expect children in England to, though maybe you would in Northern Ireland. They're not that worried about death, because in a rural community they see animals killed all the time. But some of them have seen horrific things like mutilations caused by mines. It's a good thing that they're as stable as they are.

The Bomb-Disposal Expert

Sapper Adrian Mabbott, 26, is a member of the 33rd Regiment, Royal Engineers, and is a Redfire Officer (Remote Explosive Destroyer, Falkland Islands Royal Engineers). The unit has an office in Stanley where there is a permanent display of mines, shells, grenades, missiles, mortars and rockets.

If people see something suspicious they can report it to us here and we very much welcome them coming in, because we can show them what to look for when they're out walking. Some of these exhibits are mines, others are things we get called out to see by people thinking they *are* mines. That's perfectly OK with us, we don't mind what we get called out to. These, for instance, that look like stones *are* stones, but this mine here could easily be mistaken for a pebble, specially if it's among others of that colour. We've been called out for lifting weights, wheels, even a dustbin lid.

We've had a lot of children in this morning. They keep finding rounds on the beach so we take their names and they get mentioned on the radio every fortnight. We also do talks at the school and take children down to the beach, show them a mine and blow it up by remote-control destroyers to keep them interested. We tell them never to go into the minefields and if they do find something, to mark the area and then report it to us. They're very well briefed on what to look for.

At the moment we're clearing an area that was thought to be safe but has just recently been found to contain mortars, grenades and things like that. The trouble with the minefields is that you get peat heave − when it rains, the peat soaks up water and expands, and the mines that are buried in it move too. When the peat dries, it shrinks, so they move with that as well. But we're not clearing the minefields, we've lost too many people that way − two of our officers lost feet. In the UK we're still finding bombs, mortars and mines from the Second World War, and that was over forty years ago.

I like the job, most of the people are nice, the money's better, and there aren't the terrorists there are in the UK. That's something you live with day in, day out when you're there, or you should do anyway, but you don't have to worry about them down here.

The Air-Service Manager

Peter Milner was Manager of the Falkland Islands Government Air Service (FIGAS).

The Islander aircraft fly from 500 feet to 4,000 feet and safety is the name of the game. We have to be flexible in the conditions we operate under, and pilots are used to adapting to them and making their own judgements because you can take off in sunshine and be in a snowstorm ten minutes later. I think pilots here are very special. In fact I think they are much the most skilled I have ever come across. They're not reliant on beacons and navigational aids, they have to use their own wits.

Some of the tourists can't really believe what they're seeing sometimes. They get a little bit panicky when the aircraft starts to descend and they can't see any airfield with terminal buildings and duty-free shops. We land on a grass strip in the middle of nowhere and they're quite horrified. They tap the pilot on the shoulder and say, 'What are you doing?' and he says, 'I'm landing.' I must admit it happened to me the first time.

The Councillor and Businessman

John Cheek, a fifth-generation Falkland Islander whose wife's family came over with Governor Moody in the 1840s, was a Cable and Wireless radio engineer before becoming part-owner and a director of a company involved in the fishing industry, Fortuna Ltd. John was on a visit to England during the Conflict and later spoke for the Falklands Government at the UN. He is now Chairman of the Falkland Islands Fishing Industry Association.

When the fishing business started [with the declaration of a 150-mile fishing zone around the Islands in 1986] my present colleague and I realised that Falkland Islanders could be involved in it but assumed you really had to be steeped in fishing. But then we realised there were people who weren't but were acting as middlemen for Far-Eastern companies. As my colleague said: 'If London barrow boys can do it, so can we.' We were the first to start a fishing company this way.

Now some of these Far-Eastern fishing companies are in association with us and get licences through us. We provide services like transporting the fish from fishing boat to freezer boat and then to its market, generally in the Far East. That's how we make our money. Our ultimate aim is to own our own fishing boat, but that takes awhile because there's all the capital involved. We did have a joint-venture company with Stanley Fisheries but that folded.

From the Falkland Islanders' point of view, there are two things about the fishing industry. One is the licence money that comes in to the Government, though I suspect this has now peaked because the maximum number of licences has already been allocated. And there is the danger of over-fishing, though I've heard the Falklands fishery is probably the best managed in the world. I think all of us concerned with the Falklands must want to preserve the squid rather than maximise the income, and would prefer the income to go down to a third of what it might be just to ensure that.

Why was there no fishing industry before 1986? There are 2,000 of us and we have 650,000 sheep, which means you have a tremendous number you don't want for wool, that can be eaten. I don't believe anyone could have set up a fishing business to provide for a thousand people in Stanley and compete with the price of mutton, which is 25p a pound.

The future? I don't think we could be independent but we could move towards governing ourselves more. We changed the constitution in the mid-1980s, which gave us a greater degree of self-government if only Councillors would be prepared to use it. I think they are too inward looking, more towards the past than the future. Education must be one of the main ways forward — we've lost too many good Falkland Islanders who've gone overseas to settle. I believe we must educate them to take over the professional jobs which at the moment are generally filled by those from the UK because we haven't got our own. To me, it's idiotic for Islanders to be trained and get good qualifications and not come back because the position has been filled by someone from overseas. But at the moment those on local salaries are getting, at the best, two-thirds of what those coming in will get. In the case of doctors, it's less than a third. My wife is a teacher and her salary went up above the minimum starting salary of a UK teacher for the first time in 1989, and she's been teaching for twenty years.

As long as there is any claim or possibility that Argentina would take the Islands by force, then there's a need for someone to protect us. But there are two other possibilities: one is that Argentina drops her claim and recognises the rights of the Islanders to self-determination, which is not necessarily independence. Or Britain turns round and says, 'We can no longer afford to protect you.' Either of these would break the stalemate.

The Former Chief of Police

Terry Peck, 52, a plumbing and heating engineer, was Chief of Police for twenty years before resigning in 1981. He was a member of the Government's Legislative and Executive Council from 1981 until 1984, and was re-elected in 1989. He has four children by his first marriage and a stepdaughter by his second.

I wouldn't have put money on getting re-elected but my job takes me from house to house reading electricity meters, so that keeps me in touch with people. We had seventeen candidates standing at the last election, the highest number we've ever had. My policy was that Councillors should be accountable for the use of public funds. It frightens people when they know how much money is coming in and how much being spent and wasted in lots of areas, and there doesn't seem to have been a lot of control over expenditure. Now we are endeavouring to make sure everyone is made accountable for what they do and what they spend.

So far as my work as Chief of Police was concerned, there was one woman clerk, an inspector, sergeant and four PCs – a sum total of seven. [Today there is a Force of seventeen.] I would probably like to have had two more officers – it was always difficult at public holidays and you had to double your hours to allow men to go on holiday themselves. But a great deal of support was given to the police service and I like to think I had a good relationship with the community.

Almost every morning I'd go out and walk the full length of the town and stop and chat to people or go off and have a cup of tea with some old lady or gentleman. I would take about two hours but I think it was most important to have that personal relationship with the public. When I used to walk round after the pubs were cleared at night, I'd probably come across someone I knew who was the worse for wear trying to clamber into his vehicle. You knew he wasn't intending to harm anyone so you'd just take the keys from him, push him into the passenger seat and drive him home. And if you met somebody else who was the worse for wear, you'd put him in the back of the Land Rover and take him home too. I can remember one evening taking twelve Royal Marines back to Moody Brook [near Stanley], all in the same car, when they were stoned out of their minds.

The Chief of Police

Ken Greenland served with the military police in Germany, France and Beirut before coming to the Falklands in 1983, when he retired from the army and joined the colonial police force. He is married with three children.

The establishment here is for twenty police officers. That's just enough to get by, yet one of the criticisms levelled by our local politicians is that the police-to-population ratio is too high. At the time of the war there were seven police officers but since then there's been an increase in the recorded crime rate of something like 800%. You could argue we should therefore have an 800% rise in the police force, which would bring us up to fifty officers, but we wouldn't dream of asking for that.

There is no organised crime here, no gangs, no professional villains, and we do have a very good idea of who is involved, know where we can find them and where to look for stolen goods. This has led to a 64% detection rate, which is very good – by UK standards terrific. Of the cases that actually go to court, we have a 97% conviction rate, unheard of in Britain. We get a range of crime here: assaults of various types, sexual offences, theft, though only one robbery in my five years where violence was used. No murders. I think the last was in the seventies.

The prison can hold thirteen at a squeeze and is here at the police station. It was originally built by the Royal Marines in 1873 to be the chief police officer's residence and a working station as well. I was told one Chief of Police who lived here got a prisoner to baby-sit for him.

The prison regime, in fact, is either rather harsh or extremely liberal because we only have one jailer and he has to have some time off. So if a prisoner shows himself to be unreliable, he has to go into a locked cell and stay there. We take him out for exercise but that's as much as we can hope to do. On the other hand, if he shows himself to be reliable and sensible – and there's nowhere for him to actually escape to – then he's allowed a degree of freedom which is inconsistent with him being sent to prison in the first place. In the evening when the jailer goes off duty, the outer doors are locked but the cell doors left open so the prisoner can wander up and down, make coffee and watch television. We bend visiting hours to suit visitors and it's really quite civilised as long as the prisoner behaves.

Prisoners can cut peat for old folk and do public-works-type of painting, though we don't let them do anything of a private service. I wouldn't have a prisoner come to do my garden, for example, though I believe this used to happen in the old days. If the conditions of detention are not suitable, they are sometimes sent back to England.

We've never had a woman sentenced to imprisonment since I've been here but we have had them under arrest for theft. They have a three-star cell with washbasin and loo, all self-contained and really quite comfortable. I've slept in there myself on a couple of occasions when I've been working long hours and wanted a kip.

What is absolute nonsense is that the UK driving licence isn't accepted here. This must be one of the few countries in the world where you're not allowed to drive on a foreign driving licence for at least a month or six weeks. You have to produce your foreign licence and get a Falkland Islands one for the same group of vehicles. Failing that you have to take a test, which is ludicrous. You pay £10 for a life licence, £2 for a temporary one.

A lot of people object to having the breathalyser here. Personally I think it's a very good thing because the drink problem that exists does lead inevitably to a lot of drinking and driving. We're very fortunate in that there haven't been any deaths directly attributable to drunken driving but it's a nonsense to say, 'Let's wait until there is one before doing anything about it. They talk about heavy drinking being a tradition here. It's not. It's a habit and don't think it's a way of life you should preserve. If you drive out across the Camp tracks you find every gat surrounded by broken bottles and empty beer cans. That's nothing to be proud of so far as I am concerned, it's a degree of dereliction. Again, where a farm building has burnt down, you're left with a heap of rubble, and broken down machinery is just abandoned. The Islands are a lovely place and the people themselves very nice obviously the products of this way of life. So it's a bit complex really, isn't it?

I sincerely hope one day that we'll have a local man and not an expat as head of police — it's got to be desirable. But if he's going to do the job properly he's got to be experienced and you can't get that here. I'm hoping to have an affiliation with the Devon and Cornwall Force send people there for training on specialist courses, get specialist advice when we need it and take their chaps for a year.

The Publican

A Falkland Islander, Ally Jacobsen worked in England for fourteen years as an electrician in Southampton before returning to the Falklands to run the Victory Bar. He is married and has two young children.

I came back from England because of the Victory Bar, which my father had a half share in with an Argentinian. My father died in 1980 but the Argentinian delayed proceedings to buy it and in 1982 the place was well in debt. Cathy and I decided to come back and have a go at being landlord and landlady. It's OK most of the time but we didn't realise how hard the work would be.

The pubs here are very different to the UK – they're still basically converted houses. This one's been here forty years and there used to be a sign above the door but it got broken a while ago.

We have a darts team in the League – the Globe usually win but last year we were runners-up. Cathy runs the women's team. We used to have cricket with concrete strips on the football pitch for the wicket, because even though we don't get as much rain as in England, our ground seems to hold the water a lot more – it stays muddy longer and we haven't got the time to have a proper groundsman.

We sponsored one fellow, Colin Smith, a 28-year-old carpenter, to go to Britain for the darts championships. He was winning most darts competitions here and everyone said he should go to the UK. I thought if he doesn't go, the lad's going to be disappointed, so I phoned up the British darts organisation and asked if we could enter a Falkland Islander into a British Open. It was OK so it was just a case of booking a passage and entering his name. Me and Paul Bonner paid for it – it wasn't a lot of money, just £800. He got into the last sixty-four out of over a thousand and then came up against Gary Wilson, who plays for Merseyside in Division One, and lost three straight to him. I was amazed how well he did and I think he was too.

We're open from 10 am to 1 pm and half-five to ten o'clock every weekday with a Glory Hour on Sunday. That's a total waste of time because you just get a lot of people trying to get drunk as quick as possible. When I came here about a year ago I put a carpet down and that brought an awful lot of ridicule because the general feeling was that a carpet was too good for a pub. But I haven't regretted it. It's made it a lot more comfortable. It's such a small place and the cosier I can make it the better.

I've no regrets about coming back. The thing I miss most is Radio 1. I always made a point of keeping up with pop music and it's a bit difficult here. BFBS [British Forces Broadcasting Service] do a chart programme but that's about it. I get the *Sun* and the *News of the World* to put on the bar counter but they're usually about a week old. The *Sun* costs 80p and the *News of the World* £1.10 but I think they're worth it.

We don't get many military from Mount Pleasant here because they have to sit in the back of an old three-ton lorry and get rattled round for nearly an hour, so it's not much fun for them to come into Stanley. Women don't often come in on their own but that's not looked down on now as it used to be when I was a kid. There were only certain types who came in or they were treated as such if they did.

The Deputy Head (Children's Hostel)

Lorraine McGill is Deputy Head of the hostel which houses children from Camp during term time. She lived on New Island until her marriage to Rob, and in 1974 they bought Carcass Island, where Rob now lives and to which she returns in the school holidays. They have two grown-up children.

I've been Deputy Head for two years now and was a house parent for eight years before that. At present there are thirty-four children from nine to sixteen years old with a girls' and a boys' block, and a dining room and recreation facilities in the main building. There are six house parents, two cooks, four cleaning ladies, a laundry lady, handyman and matron.

My job is to oversee the house parents, be available to children if they need me, do the accounts and ordering for the tuck shop and cope with washing machines that go wrong or any plumbing or electrical problems. I also deal with the children's pocket money, and if they cause any damage it has to be recorded and a sum asked from parents for repair or replacement.

We like to get the children out of Stanley as much as possible at weekends. Yesterday we went to Bush Pass and had a wonderful day: the children were puddling in the stream for little freshwater minnows, picking wild strawberries and going in the sea. They felt free and relaxed, it was very good.

They are homesick sometimes but I think the new telephones with private lines will make things a lot better. They can actually talk to their parents without the world and his wife hearing what they say as they used to on the radio telephone. Sometimes the older ones get cheesed off and depressed and need a little extra care and attention, and that's when the house parents come into their own. They do miss the freedom of home, where a lot of them have their own motorbikes and horses, work with farm animals, help chase the sheep, and all that sort of thing.

I think in the past Camp children have always been looked on as having straw coming out of their ears but that's dying out now. They're encouraged to invite Stanley children in for a game of darts or pool or just to sit on the lawn and chat, and local children can invite them back at weekends. We know it's nothing like home because they haven't got the wide-open spaces and the freedom but we do try and make it as relaxed and comfortable as we can, and always ask the children what they want, whether it's about pictures on the walls or the kind of outing they'd like to go on.

The Nurseryman

Tim Miller, whose family came to the Falklands as sheep farmers in the 1860s, went to school in England and took a three-year course at the Royal Agricultural College in Cirencester. He gave up sheep farming in 1988 to start a tree-nursery business and now runs a hydroponic nursery, tree nursery and garden centre.

There are not many trees in the Falklands but they d[grow if they're looked after. I planted about a thousand or the farm in my first year and sold a similar number to othe people. Then I opened a garden centre with a friend i[Stanley and it rapidly got to the stage when what was . sideline became as big as the sheep-farm business.

Although you can grow perfectly good vegetables i[gardens here and many people do, it's very difficult t[grow salad crops commercially because of the irregula summer weather. Growing something hydroponicall[[seeds are sown in little fibreglass blocks from which th[roots grow out into water that trickles beneath them] i efficient because everything is under cover and you'r[controlling the growing conditions. I've yet to mee anyone who can tell the difference in the taste of a tomat[grown this way, though it tends to have a thinner skin.

I now grow lettuce all the year round, tomatoes an[cucumber for about seven months of the year, peppers an[aubergines. We're starting to branch out into other crop[under protection and outdoors, like strawberries raspberries, cabbage, cauliflower; and root crops lik carrots, parsnips and potatoes in the fields. I'm a grea believer, with my conservative farming background, i[learning to walk before you can run and doing one thing a a time. At present I supply local markets in Stanley and ou in Camp, and we have a contract with the Ministry c Defence to supply the Forces with their salad crops. It wa a very uphill battle with the MOD because our tomatoe didn't fit the required classification and our cucumber were the wrong shape, but we managed it. The last tim the MOD inspector came down he actually said the qualit[of our goods was probably higher than anywhere in th EEC. We were quite pleased with that. We're producin[about 75,000 heads of lettuce a year, 20 tons of tomatoe and about 12 tons of cucumbers.

During the 1982 war I was living at Dunnose Head nea[Port Howard and there was an intelligence muddle by th Task Force, who got the idea that this was an Argentin[stronghold. RAF Harriers were ordered to bomb the plac and take out the airstrip, which was right alongside th[houses. They took out the airstrip but a large part of th[farm buildings as well, including very nearly me. I end[up 30 feet away from the point of impact of a thousan[

pound bomb with bits of shrapnel in my left eye. It was three weeks before I could get to the hospital ship and by that time all they could tell me was what I already basically knew, which was that I had lost the sight of that eye. The RAF pilot who dropped the bomb felt very awkward about it but I told him he was doing what he'd been told to do and as far as he knew he was destroying an enemy target. He's now a good friend.

That's one of the marvellous things about the Falkland Families Association. They're the next of kin of the servicemen who died in the war and there's a very strong bond between the Islanders and these families. We're able to talk to each other openly and can let our feelings go. Islanders do have a sense of guilt about the war. I found it very awkward when one of the wives said to me how awful it was that I had lost an eye. And I thought, How can you say this? You were widowed at twenty-one and left with two boys. How can you say that what happened to me wasn't fair? The Islanders shed as many tears at the memorial service when the families were down here as they did themselves, because we are very conscious that but for their husbands and sons we wouldn't have our country or our freedom any more. Another widow came from Northern Ireland and she said she could appreciate how we felt kind of guilty because she feels the same.

It's unfortunate that the military base was built so far away from Stanley. A lot of the servicemen come down thinking they're not going to like being here, that it's going to be cold and miserable. But others find out what's going on [outside the base] and tend to reasonably enjoy themselves. We used to have RAF pilots coming to stay with us on the farm, and others from navy ships when they were in port. Those that like it want to come back with their families but this can only be done by building more married accommodation at the base as well as back-up facilities. But you can't produce that out of a hat overnight.

The future? I can't envisage Argentina ever giving up their sovereignty claim. But if we could get away from this word 'colony', perhaps we could move to some form of recognised local autonomy, a Channel-Island or Isle-of-Man-type status. We're still very much part of Britain but could be seen to be a country in our own right. The rest of the world just doesn't understand that we are an English-speaking people, and as far as they're concerned, it's an anachronism of history. We don't want any links with Argentina. We tried commercial and trade ones once and look where that got us. But we were forced into it by successive British governments during the 1970s, who encouraged commercial relations as part of the Foreign Office ploy to woo us over to Argentina so we would become more dependent on them. They didn't want to face up to the problem and the best way was to get rid of it. You'll find very few Islanders even today have got much time for anyone from the Foreign Office. I think if the Argentine had waited another five years, they would have ended up with Britain giving them the Falklands on a plate.

The Chief Executive

Ronald Sampson is Chief Executive of the Falkland Islands' Government. He had a career in the army before going into local government in Yorkshire and Scotland.

There can't be many chief executives in Britain who can be dealing with an international matter about conserving species of squid or being involved in buying aircraft one minute, and the next sorting out someone's pension or their peat allocations – the range of things you do here is quite remarkable.

The most important issue we are looking at is the conservation of the *Illex* squid, which brings in something like 70% of the government revenue. If we can't secure the squid, the Islands' economy will be in real difficulty. The trouble with the squid is that it isn't very bright and spends half its life outside the Falkland waters where we can't easily control it. And that's where the stock can be fished out. We're trying to get agreements of voluntary restraint with the Japanese, Taiwanese, Koreans and Poles in particular, to limit the amount of fishing they do outside Falkland waters.

With regard to housing, the current policy is that the Government should not build houses but make it as easy as possible for people to build their own. We own most of the land and can make it available at a reasonable price [about £1,000 for a half-acre site] and make mortgages available at a 9% rate.

The new senior school is a very exciting project. But for A levels it would be very expensive to have teachers here with specialist knowledge for such a small number of people. I mean you're talking of a Sixth Form of only six pupils. When you consider that teacher would probably have a wife and a house and children to be sent to the UK for education, that's a huge bill. So the probability of A levels here in the near future is highly unlikely. But the success they are having with them in England and going on to university and then coming back, is quite exciting. John Barton, an Islander [Director of Fisheries], is a graduate of Bangor University and has come back to make a major contribution to the Islands. That's what we'd like to see happening more and more.

With regard to oil exploration, territorial rights have gone up from three to twelve miles and that includes land under the sea. We have drafted legislation that will allow the Government to consider whether or not they wish to go ahead with on- and offshore mineral exploration, and there are many minerals that are attractive other than hydrocarbons. I've seen offshore exploration change rural communities and not always for the best, but you always have to match that with the needs of the country. The Falklands don't need it today, but we might if the Orientals kill the squid.

Future developments? Stanley does need more variety and choice – certainly more hotel accommodation, and there could be scope for a number of businesses related to the fishing industry, like a wet-fish shop. Tourism is probably the area where you'll see the greatest growth in the next few years. Wind power has been used for many years but there are a couple of new experiments going on now. It could be used for generating electricity – at the moment electricity in Camp is in 90% of cases generated by diesel engines, and that's expensive. You have to switch them on and off, and most of the Camp goes into darkness at ten o'clock at night, which means freezers aren't running.

The new telephone system is not only going to make a difference to people already living in Camp, but makes the Falklands an attractive place to people from Europe looking for the alternative good life. You could have craftsmen, and writers who are as close to their editor at the end of the fax here as they were if living in Bermondsey. I've seen it happen in North-East Scotland where initially such people were looked on with a certain amount of suspicion in rural communities. But as time went by it was clear it was their children who were keeping the school and corner shop open and quite often it's first-generation immigrants who tend to be hyperactive and make a disproportionately large contribution to the community.

The Government has no ambition to change its current relationship with Argentina. I think the military will be here for a long time and it provides them with excellent training. There are few places in the world where they can indulge in the low flying that they do here and be welcome.

The Personal Assistant

*Maria Strange, Personal
Assistant to the Chief
Executive, is one of the very
few Argentinians living in the
Falklands. She is married to
author, artist and naturalist
Ian Strange, and has one
child, Georgina, 10.*

I came to the Falklands from the Argentine with my first husband in 1972, which was when the air-link with South America began. We came for a look, liked what we saw and decided to settle.

I was in my late twenties and thought it was a super place – it was so quaint and clean and tidy and different from Buenos Aires. It took me a long time to get used to the wind, but other than that the Britishness of it was really quite charming. The language wasn't a problem because I've spoken English since I was about five – I went to a British school and always had English-speaking friends. But I'd never been to the UK so this was my first real taste of something British.

My marriage ended after about a year here – if you have a relationship that's not going very well, living here doesn't help it. I think it's because everything becomes so intense. You can't get away and find buffers like going to a movie.

It wasn't a problem for me in the Conflict. In fact, it probably helped the local people to accept me more. Some people may have doubted whether I was going to stay and stick it out but I had no intention of leaving. This was home and there you are. It was awful, obviously, for all of us, whichever side of the fence you were on. I was so cross about the whole thing, but it was difficult later when it sank in that the links with Argentina were cut off and that meant I couldn't easily go and visit family and friends.

So many people I know in Argentina thought the whole thing was totally crazy and I think you'd find the average Argentinian still does. There may be diehard nationalistic types who would think otherwise, but on the whole most really thought it was a great waste of lives, time, effort and money.

I've been here a good seventeen years now and one gets used to the slight limitations of the place. It's only when I go back to the UK or America and see the variety and choice of things in the stores and supermarkets that I come back to Stanley and have fifty fits wondering why on earth I'm here and what am I going to eat. But it grows on you, and you survive, and I do have an interesting job.

There is so much going on in the Falklands now and it's certainly ceased being a little quiet backwater. It's got much more complicated since 1982 and Councillors are finding they have to spend more and more time on council business. Having the telephone is absolutely magic. We were recently on New Island, where the radio telephone still exists and it's friendly and comforting. I kept thinking to myself, Well, the next time we come here there will probably be a telephone, which will be lovely because we'll be able to have private conversations. But at the same time I think not having everything broadcast is going to make quite a difference to the average Camp household. If you really want to know what's going on, we say, just go out to Camp and everyone has the latest news. But Islanders are quite radio-minded and I think the radio telephone will probably still carry on.

The Environmentalist

Ian Strange, naturalist, artist, author and photographer, has worked in the Falklands for over thirty years. He is married to Maria, who comes from the Argentine. He has one son and three daughters, two by a previous marriage, and is part-owner of New Island, one of the most beautiful islands in the Falklands.

I was born in East Anglia and came down here on Christmas Eve 1959 as an agriculturist. I've always been interested in animals and the environment and farming was about as near as I could get to both. So when I was asked to come and set up an experimental farm here I jumped at the opportunity. It was initially for a three- to four-year contract, but the project was a failure economically. Though by that time I knew I loved the Islands and decided to stay.

My work since has been to do with all aspects of the Falkland environment and its wildlife, and the thing that's most important to me now is to bring all this to the attention of people outside the Islands as well as help conserve what is here. We are very small and we have to be a little bit careful. Accommodation is one constraint which is probably quite a good thing at the moment.

I bought New Island in 1971 and, two years later, started wildlife tourism there to show people that it had a certain value. The idea was and still is to establish a reserve and use it as a base for future conservation and scientific work. There's a small settlement there for visitors and for housing those who come to do various studies.

I think you have to be a particular type to survive in the Falklands. A lot come for a comparatively short time and then things get on top of them. It's quite a difficult environment – not just weatherwise – to survive in. Although you might have two aircraft flying down here every week from the UK, there's still an element of isolation. For me, the almost untouched landscape is the fascination of the place, but there are certain aspects of living with people that I find a bit difficult. I'm quite a private person in many ways and, of course, here everyone knows what your business is. When I go to the UK it's quite nice to be just somebody in a crowd.

In many ways life here is no different from England. You have your politics, big business and suffering and everything else that goes with a larger community, but there is one big difference in my view. You can see the wood in the trees, and that can be a bit disturbing because one realises that, well, take politics, there isn't the buffering effect you'd get in a large community. You know your politicians, their background, their work, the things that are hidden in large communities. Small can be beautiful but it can be disturbing because you see things in more depth.

The FIC Manager

Terry Spruce, Manager in Stanley of the Falkland Islands Company, came to the Islands thirty years ago as an office clerk on a four-year contract with the Company. He is married to an Islander. Until 1991, the FIC was the Islands' largest landowner, but it has now sold its four major farms to the Falkland Islands' Government, retaining its shipping service, retail and distribution operation, flight ticketing and construction company.

The FIC has always tended to work in the local market and encourage people to come and settle here rather than come on a specific contract – there are very few short-term posts within our operation. All salaries are based on local wage conditions so we don't have the backbiting that exists elsewhere when expats get higher wages for doing the same jobs as local people.

The FIC was incorporated by Royal Charter in 1851 and thirty years ago it owned about 45% of the total land but we started selling it off in the late 1970s. Reporting to me here are the departmental managers of the West Store, the garage, the jetty and agency, with two high-speed launches and a working launch to take stores and mail.

When I first came, the West Store was catering for 1,900 people, the permanent residents. But there are now many more of a transient nature. I'm not talking about the military but a lot more in short-term jobs. There's also been a tremendous increase in people's pockets, especially in Stanley. They now go into the West Store and buy anything they need. We also get newspapers, which we didn't before, that are only four or five days out of date.

Life in the Camp has certainly changed. People always used to think of the manager's house as the place where decisions were made. Now, with the big farms being divided up and sold, they have to make their own, and I think it's a good thing. It will sort out the wheat from the chaff and make people more aware of money, which they haven't been up to now because they haven't used it. On our farms they took a cash advance at the shop and wrote down what they bought. With the improvement in the roads, especially from Fitzroy and Goose Green, people are coming to Stanley more often and getting used to handling money.

We *have* been at loggerheads with the Government at times. They've accused the FIC of being a monopoly but no way has it been one. It's a monopolistic situation just through size, but there has always been the opportunity for someone else to come in with competition. What everyone forgets is that we are dealing with 2,000 people and it's a minute market with a minute purchasing power. It's the same as very small village shops. In fact their purchasing power could be more than ours.

There is certainly more vandalism here than there used

to be. I think it's a lack of respect for anything due to the fact that money is no object. People can change jobs and there's no unemployment. You get things now like speeding offences and stealing. One man from a merchant ship at Mount Pleasant went berserk with a knife on a military repair vessel and he's away on a plane tomorrow. The police already had a flight booked in case we did want to get rid of him.

I'd like to go back to bobby-style policing. We are not the UK, we're the Falklands and this is a unique place, so why should we have their kind of legislation? People didn't come here just for it to become a mini UK.

The Islander

Kitty Bertrand was born in Aberdeen in 1918 and spent the first eighteen months of her life there before returning to the Falklands with her parents, who were both Falkland Islands born. She lived on Carcass Island for sixteen years and when she later married her cousin Cecil, also a Bertrand, they bought the island.

When I was eight I had a governess who was Head Girl of the school in Stanley. My mother engaged her to come out and paid her the vast sum of £30 a year. She was a nice lassie — she'd just left school herself and was only sixteen. We became great friends. I think she stayed until I was thirteen, and my education was very spasmodic after that. We went to live on West Point Island and my mother eventually bought it (my brother lives there now). We had 2,400 sheep and I did mainly shepherding — I never moved without a horse.

But Carcass was my real love and I've spent the major part of my life there. You never knew exactly when the store ship was going to arrive because there wasn't any wireless to tell you, but sometimes they'd blow the hooter if it was coming from West Point, so even if you couldn't see you could hear her. If there were any letters for us, one fire would be lit on the mainland for local ones and two for English mail. We'd then light one fire if we were coming and two if we weren't, using diddledee twigs [small ground-hugging plants with red berries used for making jam] as there were no trees.

My husband was always working on boats, though he sometimes came ashore and worked on a farm. I didn't mind being completely alone in the least. Good gracious, no. When he went to New Zealand I told him it was my great ambition to stay on Carcass by myself and look after the animals, and he let me.

We were twenty-one years on Carcass and then sold it to Rob McGill who lives there now. He said we could stay on in one of the other houses there, and we did for six years before we decided it was high time we came to Stanley in case we became a nuisance. So we shipped all our goods and chattels over on our ketch *Foam*, which we'd used for getting mail from the mainland, stores from other farms and picking up the travelling teacher. When we arrived here in Stanley there were no bushes round the house and I felt exactly like a goldfish in a bowl. There are bushes now but I still miss Carcass Island terribly.

The Office Manager

Myriam Booth, who is manager of the British Antarctic Survey office, was born in Chile and came to the Falklands in 1955 when she was 12. She joined the Stanley meteorological office in 1961 and transferred to the Falkland Islands Dependency Survey, which preceded the British Antarctic Survey, in 1968. Myriam was awarded the Fuchs Medal in 1989 for twenty-eight years of 'dedicated, efficient service' and, in 1991, the MBE.

There's just me here now with a part-time helper through the summer months, which is a very busy time because the British ships come here on their way to Antarctica. This is a forward base and I am a Girl Friday, arranging accommodation for scientists flying in to join the ship and those going back home, getting provisions they require for whichever base they're going to, and sorting out their mail from Stanley post office as there are no deliveries here.

In April when the ships have gone, I'm supposed to work at the BAS headquarters in Cambridge until September. It's quite difficult working there as I'm used to being my own boss but I just do what I'm told and stay quietly out of the way, longing to get back home because I love this place. But I do enjoy shopping sprees in the UK and go mad buying furniture and food like cases of tinned tomatoes and mushrooms, and Maxwell House coffee, which I can't buy in the Falklands.

Apart from modern technology changing things here, there are social changes too. In the old days, as soon as the ships came in (the *HMS Protector* from the navy, the *Shackleton* and *John Biscoe* with BAS), there was always a dance at the Town Hall, everybody turned out and we had a marvellous time. That doesn't happen any more. You find a lot of the crew don't know the local population like they used to when the ships were crewed mainly by Falkland Islanders. Now it's all UK crew. Youngsters today don't seem that keen on going to sea. I keep putting adverts out but you don't get the response. They're more interested in fishing or contract work.

My hobby is music, rock 'n' roll, that's my era. But when the Beatles went into Sergeant Pepper and all that highbrow stuff, I thought that's not pop, that's just a noise. So I went into country music and now I do a show every Thursday night on FIBS [the Falkland Islands Broadcasting Station] called *Pot Luck*.

The Tourist Officer

Graham Bound, 33, is Managing Director of the Falkland Islands Tourist Board. He is a fifth-generation Falkland Islander, and one of his ancestors came out in 1843 with Governor Moody, who founded Stanley two years later.

We had a thriving tourist industry before 1982 but of a different nature to that which exists today. Large cruise ships carrying up to 1,000 passengers would disgorge hordes of people into Stanley maybe five or six times a season and they'd ransack the shops and buy everything. It's essentially a free port except for alcohol and cigarettes but even the duty is quite light. There were regular supply ships from Buenos Aires and a twice-weekly air service from South America which brought a steady stream of groups throughout the year. This kind of tourism didn't change the face of the Islands at all but it could be a bit of a cultural shock to residents to have hundreds of people coming in at any one time, and not consistent with the life they wanted to lead.

Now we're getting tourists moving round the Islands more and requiring accommodation, and we've created a five-year strategy which allows for a growth of up to 500 land-based tourists a year. These are the people who come on package tours and spend two weeks touring the Islands. But FIGAS [the Falkland Islands Government Air Service] has only got three 8-seater aircraft and can only fly so many hours, and if shearers can't get about it can be a problem. There's also the domestic trade and the cruise ships, the bulk from which is now very substantial.

What we want to do is spread the domestic business over a much longer season, and we've started a Valentine's Package at Port Howard and a Christmas Special at Pebble Island.

What do tourists do in the Falklands? There's wildlife and wilderness, spectacular concentrations of birds and sea mammals, world-class trout fishing, land yachting, good hiking, horse-riding, golf and even a bit of camping. There have been reports that there's been some damage from helicopters coming into sensitive areas and photographers walking into penguin colonies, and we do need to establish certain codes of conduct because tourism in a place like this has the capacity to destroy the very thing it's selling.

We're hoping that there will be links with Chile quite soon, which would be very good for tapping into the American market because from our research we know US tour operators are interested.

I would very much like to have a ship going round the

different islands but we had our failure in that area unfortunately. The *Southern Star*, which we tried to introduce, failed because the Government made the strategic decision not to be involved in this kind of commercial tourism. It would have been well worth a subsidy to my mind. The islands in the west are beautiful but very difficult to get to, and it would take the pressure off FIGAS too.

The Customs Officer and Harbour Master

Les Halliday, a third-generation Falkland Islander, started his working life at 15 as a messenger and filing clerk for the Secretariat, the administrative authority. He is married to Peggy and was instrumental in starting the Falklands' flourishing philatelic business.

LES: We have to clear any aircraft and ships coming into the colony and check all the passenger baggage from tourists and military personnel on the Tristar. We also have to see if there are any dutiable goods on cargo ships like beer, wine, spirits, tobacco, cigars, cigarettes, but otherwise it's a free port.

I couldn't put my hand on my heart and say there are no drugs in the Falklands because I'd be a fool if I did, and we've got to be vigilant. One of my staff has been away on a three-month training course which included drugs, because eventually I'm sure they will come.

We have cruise ships stopping here and passengers go round Stanley and look at the shops. But no ship should bring any Argentinians into the Falklands. In fact, ships shouldn't come from an Argentine port. All supplies are brought through the Falkland Islands Company, and Hogg Robinson bring in mainly military cargo. The *Monsunen* carries cargo and wool, and the *Forrest* supplies all the farms with freight. We have the *Indiana* to take passengers from Montevideo and Punta Arenas in Chile and it brings in fruit, vegetables and timber.

I'm a churchwarden and we've launched an appeal for a million pounds to restore the cathedral, which has its centenary in 1992. It needs a new roof, all the windows have to be taken out and the brickwork has worn away with the wind and the rain. The Government has said they will give us £50,000 this year and next, and will match us pound for pound. There was a service in the cathedral when the families who had lost relatives in the war were down here. I think they were very happy with the way people looked after them, and were much easier in their minds when they found out where their loved ones had died and what they died for. We'll be for ever thankful and grateful to them. Quite a few of the military from Mount Pleasant come to our house every Sunday after the evening service in the cathedral – they love it here though a lot would be much happier if they could bring their families to the Falklands. I don't think I'd stay if the military was taken away. I'd go to England. And Heaven forbid if oil is discovered. We'd get a certain element working on it, and prostitution and drunks and everything like that. It's the last thing I want for this place. If we can survive without oil, I'm all for it.

With regard to fishing and the 'voluntary restraint' imposed on fishing vessels [a limit on the amount of squid caught outside the protection zone], I don't know if any countries actually keep to it. They know the tricks of the trade and cover up the names of their boats. I think our patrol boats are probably too slow to catch them, and if they're fishing outside the zone, there's nothing we can do about it because it's not within our jurisdiction.

PEGGY: My first job in the morning is to feed our five cats and the hens. I clean the house and sometimes do a little bit of weeding but Les does the garden. On Tuesdays I go to the Day Centre for Senior Citizens after lunch, and we have a social evening once a month with bingo and other games. I'm Chairman of the Red Cross and we're just going to get involved with 'Practise for Disaster' plans. I know it sounds a bit gloomy but if a plane crashed at Mount Pleasant it would be more than the hospital could cope with and we could be flown out to help with the less injured and comfort people. We also have the Corona Society which welcomes new people to the Islands.

Four families take it in turns to have people from Mount Pleasant back after church on Sunday nights. Sometimes they bring a guitar and have a sing-song but that's usually at someone else's house because we don't want to upset our neighbours. They said they wouldn't be, but when you're living close like we are, you've got to respect them.

The West Store is much better than it used to be, though they do run out now and again. Ice cream is an absolute luxury and costs about £3 for a two-litre pack. Marmalade is about £1 a jar. Things are getting more expensive.

The Canon

John Gervais Maurice Walker Murphy was born in Bangor, County Down, in 1926 and played rugby for Ireland. He was Domestic Chaplain to the Queen when Rector of Sandringham from 1980–87. Canon Murphy came to the Falklands in 1987 for five years. He is married and has five daughters. His parish, the largest in the world, covers the Falklands, South Georgia and the Antarctic.

We do miss our family but believe it is part of our vocation to come here. The Archbishop of Canterbury wanted someone to go and it didn't appear too easy to find anybody. There were a number of things that seemed to indicate it was the right thing for me. We had been in the Norwich diocese for almost thirteen years, living and working in small villages and farming communities that seemed to have the same lifestyle as these islands. I had also been a soldier in the Irish Guards and had twenty-five years in the Forces.

When this was a diocese stretching out to the whole of South America including Chile, Peru and Argentina, the Bishop had his seat here in Stanley. Regrettably this contact stopped in 1977 and the seal was put on that in the 1982 Conflict. So our link today is directly with the Archbishop of Canterbury, and his representative comes down to hold communion services. The cathedral is very large and takes 400 people, with a squeeze, on occasions like Liberation Day and Battle Day.

A typical day? Like most clergy, one deals with personal matters in the morning, starting with morning prayer and devotions from about 7.15. I normally go to the cathedral and when we don't have communion service I make private devotions and am always joined by my wife. We read prayers together for the Islands, the people and the world. This is a very real part of our day – to present, in prayer, the things we believe are in front of us and ask for this gift of wisdom and understanding in how to deal with them.

I go to the junior and infants school at nine o'clock and talk to children and then there are visits to the hospital. If there's a bereavement or a death, or a crisis, or an accident at sea, one gets involved in all that kind of thing. Problems here aren't very different from those in Norfolk. The securities available to people through faith in God are just as real as they are in any other part of the world.

One thing is different, though, to an English village. We have a situation where people are elected to positions of leadership to decide about roads, water, electricity and telephones, all pretty local-parish stuff. But at the same time these islands are a colony, very much part of the British Commonwealth, and local leaders not only need to be concerned about the texture of the roads but also have to go and sit in the United Nations and take part in world affairs. It's quite a demanding thing and the people have all my respect in the way they manage to do that.

In October 1991 Canon Murphy returned to the UK. He is now chaplain of the Royal Chapel of St Peter Avincula at the Tower of London.

The Telephone Operator

Hilda Perry, 58, a second-generation Falkland Islander, was an operator at the old telephone exchange (for calls within Stanley) from 1963 until 1989, when the new telephone system was introduced, enabling calls to be made throughout the Islands. She was awarded the British Empire Medal for continuing to work though the Argentine invasion and much of the occupation.

There were about 400 lines when I started work and we finished up with about 600. During normal working hours there were two operators on duty Monday to Friday, but at weekends there was just one and you had to handle the lot, which was heavy going. After '82 we got much busier and had five staff working on a three-day shift. When there was an emergency in the night we all had to go and help and sometimes, even though I'm not working there any more, I still find myself heading for the door when the fire alarm goes off. I used to run across to the telephone exchange, clothes on inside-out and back to front.

People were supposed to ask for the numbers they wanted when they rang in, but Islanders move around so much it was very difficult to keep our telephone directory up to date. More often than not they'd ask for the person by name and if he or she wasn't at home, we'd probably have seen them walking down the road or going into the West Store, so we'd just tell the caller where they were. There were a lot of party lines with the same telephone number and we had to ring three times to get one person and four times to get their neighbour. Government House had different room numbers in our directory for the Pink Room, Blue Room and Green Room.

People used to ask for all kinds of information. Where do flowers go for a funeral? What time does the funeral start and where does it take place? Or we'd get asked how to spell something. None of us were scholars or knew how to spell very well but, if we didn't know, we'd say we'll ring so-and-so for you, they'll know. We were like an information bureau as well as a telephone exchange.

If old people had any problems they'd ring us and if we couldn't help them, we could always find someone who would. If they wanted transport and couldn't think who to contact, well, they'd ring us up and we'd contact someone we knew had a vehicle.

I remember spending one evening talking to a young woman – she'd phoned in and was a bit distressed and maybe just wanted someone to talk to. I had to keep answering calls and say 'Just a minute' and then go back and speak to her again until someone else rang. I think I chatted to her for about two hours at least. I suggested putting her through to someone else but she didn't want anyone else. She had a stepdaughter who was playing up badly and was worried about what she should or shouldn't do. Not that I could really advise her, but I just let her talk, and that was the main thing that helped her, I think. It's not always easy to talk to your neighbour or one of your family. Sometimes you just want to chat to someone outside.

The Director of Education

Phyllis Rendell, 41, a first-generation Falkland Islander, went to school and college in Britain. She came back in the seventies to teach, and met and married Mike, a Royal Marine, now owner of the Malvina House Hotel. They have one son.

It was quite a difficult decision to apply for this job and I'm the first Islander to fill it. You lack confidence in a small place with everyone watching you, but I had a lot of encouragement from the then Chief Executive, who said, 'Go on and have a go.' In the early 1980s we didn't have much of an infrastructure in Camp education, and the travelling teachers weren't qualified but recruited from wherever we could get hold of them. But we felt Camp children (there are about sixty of them) deserved the same quality of teaching as those in Stanley and now we have a team of six, who come on a one-year contract. You can't really expect people who are living out of a rucksack and no permanent home to come for longer than that, but those who have a bright, positive attitude have a wonderful time and I think they go away with very fond memories.

A travelling teacher visits a family for two weeks in every six, and the weeks when they're not there, the children have lessons from a radio-school centre with both radio and travelling teachers working closely together. The children develop very warm relationships with them and feel quite privileged that this grown-up comes specially to see them. The teacher gets involved with their animals, the farm, going out and exploring – it's a very positive relationship. On the larger farms, we have teachers living and working there permanently, but with the subdivision of many of these in 1982, their population has declined and more children are scattered in remote areas where young couples have bought their own farms. Some children are very confident on the radio because they use it to talk to Mum or Dad or Grandma; others are a bit shy so we feed them in when they're ready.

Children from Camp come to Stanley at about eleven at the top end of the junior school or first year of the senior school, and they stay in the hostel. At fifteen (we hope to raise the leaving age to sixteen when the new school is built) those who want to take A levels – about six a year – go to the Peter Symonds' College at Winchester in England. Some get very homesick. Last year we had a couple who felt pretty miserable and we had to do a lot of coaxing, with their parents telling them to be sensible and not throw up the opportunity they had, and they did get through it.

We Islanders want to see young people come back with qualifications and take up some of the key posts to replace

A holiday cottage on Carcass Island; the surrounding trees are a rare sight in the Falklands.

The Pink Shop, Stanley, known as the Harrods of the Falklands, sells gifts, books, artists' materials and locally made knitwear.

Following page
Top left   Jubilee Cottages, Stanley
Top right   Christchurch Cathedral, Stanley was built in 1892 and is the most southerly cathedral in the world. The whalebone arch, made from the jawbones of a blue whale, was put up in 1933 to commemorate the centenary of the Falklands as a British colony.
Bottom left   Poppy Napier with some albatross chicks on West Point Island. She and her grandparents Roddy and Lilly are the island's only inhabitants.
Bottom right   Goose Green, 60 miles from Stanley, and the second-largest population centre, has one of the biggest shearing sheds in the world. Here, at shearing time, Brook Hardcastle (*right*), former General Farm Manager, gets the day's work organised with Tony McMullen.

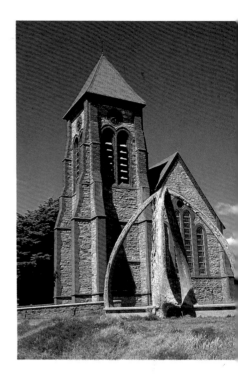

An 8-seater Britten-Norman Islander aircraft, one of three provided by the Falkland Islands Government Air Service, lands on rough grass after the sheep have been cleared away. About thirty grass and beach airstrips serve almost all the Islands' settlements.

Port Howard Airport. No waiting problems here. The pilot of an incoming plane is in radio contact with the farmer on the ground and passengers drive to the airstrip about fifteen minutes before the plane is due to land.

Port Howard is home to about forty people and 42,000 sheep. Tourists come here to enjoy the fishing, walking and horse-riding on the 200,000-acre farm settlement.

There are no traffic jams on this 35-mile-long road linking Stanley to Mount Pleasant Airport, but its uneven surface demands a 40 mph speed limit.

In January 1990 Islanders arrived by horse, Land Rover and helicopter to celebrate the 300th anniversary of the first landing in the Falklands, made by Captain John Strong in his ship the *Welfare*.

Shepherds on horseback at North Arm Farm set out to round up sheep for shearing.

those sent down from Britain. But we should also encourage other people who want to make the Falklands their home to come too, because you can't expect young Islanders to come back and stay for ever. They might want to have experience somewhere else. We'd like to see a lot more Falkland Islands nurses and teachers here but we do very well with pilots – boys are attracted to this. Local administration lacks young Islanders and we should make it more attractive for them to go into it. There's quite a range of jobs here now – much more than fifteen years ago when it was just farming and teaching.

But the area I really want to see move now is further education for those who haven't gone on to do A levels. There's a whole group of very useful citizens who we're not doing enough for, and I feel we need to develop their skills in technology and basic building skills. We don't want them to feel failures because they don't go off to do A levels. I want them to feel successful in their own way too.

The Hotelier

Mike Rendell came to the Falklands as a Royal Marine in 1974, married Phyllis, a Falkland Islander, and after fourteen months returned to Britain. He left the Marines in 1976 and worked in Saudi Arabia and other parts of the world. Mike returned to the Falklands in September 1982 and worked for the Government as an administrator. He bought the seven-bedroom Malvina House Hotel in 1983.

Some people ask how we can continue to call the hotel Malvina House. Well, the building was built twenty years ago but the original Malvina House was here for a hundred years before that. It hasn't got an 's' on the end, which the Argentines use for the Falklands, and it's also a local girls name. If you change the name of the hotel, are all these ladies going to change their names as well? We're not a banana republic where they do this sort of thing.

The supply of food for the hotel is a very difficult problem because you can't guarantee continuity. Most o the fish we serve is caught locally so we're quite well off in terms of squid, cod, mullet and mussels, but I very rarely serve mutton, which a lot of people think is all that *is* eaten in the Falklands, because it's difficult to get here in Stanley and the quality can't be guaranteed. I serve lamb which is younger than it would be in the UK and is easier to get because the animals are lighter and you can bring them in in the aircraft. The bigger mutton have to come by sea so you're dependent on a ship going to the right farm at the right time and the farmer being in a position to stop shearing and kill some for you.

We get fruit and vegetables every two or three weeks on the *Indiana* from Chile and we're really going back to the situation twenty or thirty years ago when the *Darwin* used to run to Montevideo once a month. But that was taken away and we had to rely on an air-link with Argentina.

Mike was one of three candidates to stand in the last election for a new 'Desire the Right' party, which aimed to give people more of a say in local affairs. The title comes from the Falkland Islands' motto and was the name of the ship owned by John Davis, the first man to sight the Islands in 1592.

There's a lot of superstition in the Falklands about party system, which I find difficult to understand. With the financial responsibility now being taken locally, on would have thought it would be a good idea to have as many people involved in making policies as possible because as individuals some of us were extremely frustrated with what seemed to be a lack of decision being taken by our Council.

There was a lot of misunderstanding during the election about the party's stance on ties with the Argentine because the Desire the Right advocated discussion between Argentina and Britain on the conservation o fisheries outside Falkland waters. Some of the media here misinterpreted us and took the opportunity to twist things slightly to make the electorate believe we actually countenanced a dialogue with Argentina, which was far from the case. A lot of people feel there should be trade with Chile or Uruguay, but I don't think there are many who would want anything to do with the Argentine. It is important Britain and Argentina get back together: they need trade between each other and there are traditional links too. But please leave the Falklands out of it.

If there is to be any change at all it should be for our independence, but the great problem is defence, and guarantees would have to be reached to ensure we didn't get any other incursions from Argentina. But unless we start talking about other options, it will just grind on as it is. Everyone is very happy with the current situation with the UK, and no way would they want to change if they could guarantee it was going to go on for ever. But sometimes I, as a newcomer, find it difficult to accept the siege mentality when all the time you're looking over your shoulder to see what the UK Government is doing and what's going to be the situation when there's a General Election.

The Retired Financial Secretary

Harold Rowlands is a second-generation Islander whose grandfather, a Swedish sailor, was shipwrecked in the Falklands and remained as a skipper. Harold joined the Treasury in 1948 and became Financial Secretary in 1974. In the years until his retirement in 1989, the Falklands' revenue increased from £3 million to £30 million, most of which was brought in from the sale of fishing licences. He was elected a Councillor in 1989 and is now a member of the eight-strong Legislative Council.

Dealing with £3 million was a great deal more worrying than £30 million. We had to try and balance the budget and squeeze everything out of so little. But I believe the Government did get their priorities right after the war when they decided to improve the electricity and water supplies first.

The priority now for the benefit of people in Camp and Stanley is education and I think building the new senior school is the next large project to tackle. There's also been pressure from those in Camp to improve the tracks between the settlements. I don't think we can go ahead with any vast scheme, because it's not economic, but there is room for improvement on social grounds so that people can travel by road instead of air. It will mean a great change of life for those in the settlements.

People are very shy round here and although they have some very good ideas, they don't come forward if they fee they've got to stand up in public. I find it's often more effective to sit down and have a talk with them on their own. I'm Chairman of the Fisheries Advisory Policy Committee and a lot of people are coming to see me about that. Licences are granted by the Director of Fisheries and one of our jobs is to make recommendations as to who should have them. What we look for most is to make sure the particular project will be beneficial to the Falklands.

I suppose the most complaints I get as a Councillor are about the dental service because there's only one dentist and he is unable to cope with the workload, but we're trying to get a locum down to assist in the fisheries' busy period.

The Taxi Driver

Jane McEachern

It was a funny thing that made me start up a taxi service. I was actually doing cashier work in the West Store, working at the Victory Bar at nights and doing laundry work for contractors to make enough money to get on my feet again after being widowed. Then I was in a road accident. I'd hitched a lift to Mount Pleasant because my wee boy was in the Scouts and I wanted to see him on parade, but the guy who was driving turned the Land Rover over and I got crushed and was in a right mess.

I wasn't supposed to work for three months, so I lost my West Store job and had to give up the pub because I couldn't hold anything with one hand. The only thing I could do was carry on with the laundry, because I could hold the clothes with my teeth and take them up with the other hand. My dad was very good and came to see me and asked if I'd ever go back on the road again. And I said I'd *never* get back in a vehicle where somebody else was driving. I said I'd drive myself or not go anywhere. So he went fifty-fifty with a Safari and asked what I was going to do with it. I said, 'Make it work and start a taxi service.'

Now it's work seven days a week and when the bus service disappears they all phone me up to carry on, and it's the same at Christmas if the hospital drivers want to disappear. 'Oh, Jane doesn't need to cook her Christmas lunch, she'll run everyone home, wheelchairs and all, you know.'

The FIDC Manager

Mike Summers, whose family arrived in the Falklands in the 1840s, won a scholarship in 1964 to a boys' grammar school in Britain. He took a business studies course at Middlesex Polytechnic and worked in engineering for contracting companies around the world before returning to the Falklands in 1989 at the age of 36 to become General Manager of the Falkland Islands Development Corporation. He is married to Nicola, a government information officer.

Going to school in England was so exciting I didn't notice how much of a plunge it was and that I wouldn't be coming back for a holiday for two years. It was probably more difficult for my parents than for me.

But ever since I was away I was looking for an opportunity to come back to something I really wanted to do. I wasn't prepared to be a schoolteacher or a farmer and it's taken until this time to find something that really appealed to me. The work I'm doing now gives me the opportunity to do a job that is interesting and challenging and contributes to the development of the Falklands. It's an ideal combination.

The FIDC was set up by the British Government in 1983 and has been funded by the Overseas Development Administration in the UK with about £7 million of the £31 million grant given to the Falklands in 1982. Its purpose was to seek ways for Islanders to earn money from sources other than farming, because up until that time, that was the only source of revenue. Since then we've taken an active part in the land-reform programme by creating the mechanism for subdivision purchase and owner occupancy for farmers. The big advantage of this is that it keeps money in the Falklands instead of, as in the past, the profits being sent to the farms' external landlords. We've also made provision for mortgages and given farmers grants for areas of capital investment neglected by old landowners.

We've set up four Tourist and several self-catering Lodges in the Camp and are responsible for getting tourists down here from the UK. There's a minimum number of people needed to make them financially viable, and we haven't reached this yet but are hopeful that by next year the Lodges will begin to become profitable enterprises, which is another way of getting money out of Stanley into the Camp. The new fishing industry only brings in revenue to central government and little filters through to the business community in general, and none of it out to the Camp.

On the agro-industrial side, we've been responsible for setting up Stanley Poultry, an egg-production unit, the Falkland Mill at Fox Bay, a pilot project to rear salmon, a market garden in Stanley, as well as taxi, bus and haulage businesses. We've built an industrial estate that houses building and decorating companies, a garage and the Falkland Farmers Co-operative. We've helped accountancy and legal services to be set up here and made enterprise grants for people to start really small-scale businesses.

The success rate? Since the Corporation was set up there has never been a detailed record kept of the results and we're now looking through the grants, loans, hire-purchase arrangements and equity investments to see exactly how much we have contributed to the gross national product.

There have been a few failures with some of the enterprises but I've now reorganised the Corporation very substantially. It was overstaffed in some junior areas and understaffed in senior ones and it lacked the necessary business skills to run properly. Financial records were very poorly kept and we had a tremendous struggle to bring all that information up to date.

We're not having any more experts down from the UK at present — we have sufficient knowledge and expertise ourselves to be able to deal with most of the problems we have. One of these, in the past, was that expensive consultants would come here and tell us what we knew already — the ability they had was to be able to write it all down, put it in a bound report and give it back to us. Now we can do these things for ourselves.

I think it's a bit of a shock to people when they come here to see the amount of work there is to be done. You come imagining it to be a small, quiet little backwater but it's far from that — the pace of business in the Government and private enterprise is tremendous and much faster than in the UK or anywhere else I've been. That's since 1982, of course, and until now the changes have really only affected Stanley to any great extent, although there has been a change in structure in ownership terms.

One of the things we plan to do in the future is to sponsor bringing down a herd of goats for experimental use. The purpose is twofold: one is that we believe goats can have a significant impact on pasture improvement because they'll eat things sheep won't, like diddledee berries and the Christmas bush. If they eat those in preference to grass and leave that for the sheep, they will provide an alternative cash crop because you can comb them and sell the fibre.

There are loads of things to do – the problem is finding good people to do them. We would like more to come down in a steady and controlled fashion because we wouldn't be able to cope with a large influx of new people. It has to be the right kind of person and that's someone who is basically self-sufficient.

There are some very special qualities that I like about the Falklands: it's very easy to find peace and quiet in the countryside, to see wildlife basically undisturbed and to be able to walk over a hill and not see anyone else at all. People coming for the first time do miss the ability to pop out to the shops, but after a period of time you get used to that as well.

The Newspaper Editor

Jim Stevens worked as a production journalist on national newspapers in Britain before coming to the Falklands in 1989 as editor of Penguin News, *the Islands' fortnightly newspaper.*

The name *Penguin News* sounds a bit funny to people outside but it's what Islanders know and are used to. I'm feature writer, compositor, advertising manager, circulation manager, and do everything, in fact, except for the printing, which is done by government printers.

I think there could be a tremendous difficulty being editor if I was a true blue expat but I am a Bennie-in-law [Bennie is the disparaging name given to the Islanders by the military, from the character in the TV soap opera *Crossroads*], which makes a big difference on the cocktail circuit, and I'm accepted by the locals because they accepted my son, who is married to an Islander and was a farmer here before the Conflict.

We don't actually publish our circulation figures but there are 2,000 people and we can guarantee to get the paper to every household. We also have a fluctuating sale at the Mount Pleasant barracks. We're financed at the moment by the Government but The Media Trust acts as a buffer between us, and I don't feel there are really any problems.

I don't think the voluntary restraint policy on the fishing is working but I can't actually prove it because the figures I've got differ from those the Government have given me, and short of hiring a ship or plane and going out and looking for myself, I'm not going to know. The main difficulty is that there's only me and there isn't time to interview people in an investigative way as well as produce the paper

Port Howard

Port Howard Farm on West Falkland is so large no one knows exactly how big it is, but it's thought to cover around 200,000 acres, with 44,000 sheep and 800 cattle. It was founded in 1866 by James Lovegrove Waldron and his brother, who then went to live in Patagonia and left the farm to be managed locally. Robin and Rodney Lee bought it in 1986 and employ about forty people, many of whom own shares in the new company.

Port Howard has one shop that opens twice a week and sometimes has the atmosphere of a party, for on Fridays the whole community comes not only to stock up but to meet each other. A small shed has been turned into a little museum for relics of the Argentine war, with kit bags, an ejector seat and pistols among the items on display. An 'Ode to Tumbledown', a poem by An Unknown Scots Guard, is pinned to the wall.

Today many tourists come to Port Howard, one of the prettiest of the settlements with its green-roofed houses and almond-scented hedges edging the fields. They can watch sheep rounded up by a motorcycling shepherd and see them sheared; catch sea trout on a wide stretch of the Warrah River; go riding or walk across fields to where Captain John Hamilton lies buried in a small white-fenced cemetery on the side of a hill. His bravery in the war so impressed the Argentinians that they asked for a Union flag to cover his body, and this was done.

The Farm Company Manager

Robin Lee, 42, is joint-owner of Port Howard Farm and General Manager of Falklands Landholdings Ltd. A fourth-generation Falkland Islander, he was brought by his mother on horseback from Fox Bay to Port Howard when he was a few weeks old. Members of the Lee family have been head stockmen in Port Howard since 1890, and when his father died, Robin and his brother Rodney became managers. In 1986 they bought the 200,000-acre farm from its UK owners and encouraged employees to take shares in the new company. Robin is divorced and has two sons and a daughter. He was a Councillor for four years and ran the Tourist Lodge at Port Howard before becoming General Manager of Falklands Landholdings Ltd, a private company that owns 27% of the farmland in the Islands. At

When I was a boy I always dreamt of going abroad and I went to work on the Stanley-to-Montevideo mailboat before going to study sheep farming in New Zealand. Before then I'd never used a telephone or been in a lift, and I got my international driving licence in Stanley without ever having seen a traffic light.

The Lee family were always very much the people with the sheep. Head shepherds and the like. My grandfather came out in 1870 and worked as a shepherd, probably starting when he was about twelve years old, and he knew every nook and cranny of Port Howard. Some days I think it would be nice to go and wake him up and say, 'Come and have a look.' I think he'd be really proud but a bit shocked that we'd had the cheek to even suggest we ought to buy the farm from the bosses. I can remember even my aunt being a little shocked too. She's really proud now but I did detect this sort of tut-tutting that we should think of owning the place.

There are lots of stories about the old shepherds but I remember there was one who had a very basic house with outside loo, no running water, and if you wanted a wash you got yourself a bucket of water from the well and added a bit of hot to it. But he used to provide really good food. One of the things he did was offer you a drink before you had your meal, and he always went to his drinks cupboard and opened it about two inches and said to everyone 'What would you like, some of this, some of that or some of the other?' And nobody really knew what he had in there but we all knew he had some rum so we said, 'A tot of rum would be nice, Sandy,' and off he'd go and give you one. We never knew if he had a variety of drinks in there or there was only rum anyway. In my day no one ever dared ask him.

Port Howard is still a company-owned farm, it's just that the shareholders actually live here. Our head shepherd is friends with nearly all the youngsters who have bought their own farms. He hasn't done so himself but he reckons he's as well off as they are. He goes and visits them and sees them working seven days a week and not able to afford to draw much in the way of wages. They're all happy, but *he's* sitting there with his brand-new Land Rover, a nice house with a vegetable garden, his peat all provided for and his meat's there every week, as much as he wants for *present the Government is the sole shareholder but it is hoped that shares will be sold to Islanders in the future.*

free. His wife wanders over to the dairy for milk and they're quite happy with their life. He works hard but it's only a five-day week and then he goes off fishing or for long holidays. The only thing at the end of the day is that he won't have a piece of land, but he doesn't particularly want one.

Running a farm in the Falklands is nothing like running one in the UK. You have to be involved with the social side of people's lives, helping them when they're ill, when they have marriage problems or are just fed up. I've been a magistrate for the day, married people and had to find punishments for those committing crimes. If it's stealing, you usually ask the person to apologise and return what's been taken or threaten to dismiss him. It seems to work.

It's a bit like being a ship's captain, you really are responsible for everyone and it's on your mind all the time. Sometimes I don't think people realise the kind of strain it puts you under. You can see a lot of young lads having a great time tearing around on motorbikes, and the thought that runs through my mind is, I hope they don't collide with one another because it will be me who has to pick up the pieces.

What we need to do in Port Howard now is expand. I think the infrastructure – the water supply and electricity – could cope with at least eighty more people. We employ a number of young men, but there's no social life for them as you seldom see a female. I think we should have more people with different interests. Nearly everyone is involved in farming and it would be nice to have someone running a store or making jewellery. I'd also like to see people building homes for their retirement, because at the moment, once you can't work any more you have to go and live in Stanley, and elderly people are really missed in the community. Lack of housing is a big problem. We have no wood and buildings have to be imported in kit form.

The most contentious issue now is how do we invest the money from the fisheries? Do we put it into more fishing activities or into agriculture? Do you ignore hard business facts and look at the social side, or go ahead and make lots of money? That may make a lot of businessmen and fishing people rich, but will it make the Islands a good place to live in? I've dreamt for years about getting a ferry between East and West Falkland, and at last we are going to get one.

At present the only way to get to Stanley from here is to fly and that costs £60 return — a lot of money to go to town for the day, and that's only for one person.

Islanders themselves are not sure what they feel about the future. They want the good things in life but at the same time don't want life to change.

It's still the sort of place for people who are into self-sufficiency — you have to cut your own peat for heating and cooking, make your own bread, butter and cheese, grow your own vegetables. And it's certainly for those who like getting away from it all. If I went to the middle of the farm, I could guarantee there'd be nothing and no one for fifteen miles. A hundred and fifty years ago there were no people at all — just wild foxes.

The Book-keeper

Ron Reeves, 43, is book-keeper at Port Howard settlement and Poet Laureate of the Falklands, a title conferred on him by the BBC when he won a poetry competition in their twice-weekly Calling the Falklands *programme.*

I used to work for Haringey Council in London and then I got this urge to be a farmer. The nearest I got to it then was working in a hospital garden but I had a subscription to *Farmers Weekly* and saw this advert for a job in the Falklands. So I wrote away and one thing led to another and in 1966 my brother and I set sail from London. It took thirty-two days to get here, chugging along in a little cargo boat. We stopped once at Las Palmas, then next stop Stanley.

We'd got accommodation in a cookhouse and did just general farm jobs. I took to it straight away but my brother hated it. A hell of a lot of people take one look at the Falklands and they're off, but I fell in love with it. It's got to be something in you to live in a small community, and I had it. I was never homesick, though sometimes lying in my room on a Sunday morning, I could imagine I was home. But I didn't have a circle of friends to miss, only people I worked with. I used to write to my parents every week but they've never been here – it's far too costly.

I did the four years I'd come for, shearing sheep and tractor driving, and worked hard at trying to acquire some skills, but in 1970 I got paid off and sent home. I found I just couldn't settle in England, it was like being put out to civvy street. Here you're completely looked after by the farm. They deal with your money and the cooking's done for you – some of it's a bit ropy but you're not going to starve. It's a very paternal system, though that side's fading now.

So in 1972 I came back to the Falklands. And I got ambitious. I decided I wanted to be a gardener up at the Big House and get away from shearing. I like the sunshine and you lose all your best weather in the shearing shed.

I got the job, married a local girl, everything was rosy and I stayed there thirteen years until I fell out with the boss and got the sack.

All sorts of things were going wrong at that time. The Conflict was very traumatic: it tipped up all your values. Before then you only had the occasional visitor. Suddenly you had 1,000 military coming through. They set up a Services Adventure Training Unit just a hundred yards from our house and we had all the razzmatazz that goes with it. I got pretty fed up and started to write. It was daft stuff, but it kept me busy. Then I won the BBC poetry prize and that really surprised me.

Now I work in the office here and go on long thirty-mile walks most weekends. The land is untouched except for sheep fences and they're soft on the eye. There's about 13,000 acres per person out here and nowhere else in the world that you'd get that, not where it's safe to live. One old chap said they should give the Falklands to the World Wildlife Trust. That would be nice but it wouldn't suit a lot of people who want to develop the land and have a higher standard of living. People in the UK have this, I know, but I think they've lost a lot of other things in the process.

The Schoolteacher

Dennis Humphreys, a former animal technician, came from London in 1974. He was employed as a shepherd by the Falkland Islands Company and later qualified by correspondence course as a Montessori teacher. His wife Margaret comes from Eastbourne and their two children were born at Port Howard.

The Government like the idea of having teachers out in Camp because it encourages families to move back to the settlements. At present there are four children in the school here – three 6-year-olds (one is mine) and an eight-year-old, and I teach another eight- and a nine-year-old by radio. We have a full school day starting at nine and finishing at half-past three with smoko [buns and coffee] at half-ten to eleven.

The children get on very well as a small unit but they're also very open when another child spends a day at school. I recruit anyone interesting who comes here to give a talk. I let the children choose their own subjects of a morning, and this year they did a play at Christmas which they thought up themselves. It was *Four Little Pigs* – it had to be four. But my two radio students came down so we managed to have a penguin narrator, a wolf and four little pigs. Once that was finished, they had a pop concert, made their own guitars, tie-dyed their gowns, and the whole settlement came to see it.

I'm in contact with my radio pupils for half an hour every day, though sometimes it's three-quarters of an hour. You try to work with them and the classroom children at the same time, with a lot of nature-study-type quizzes which they can all be involved in.

Much of the success of radio teaching depends on parents, who have to make sure the children are there on time otherwise they miss me. I'm sometimes teaching them when the others come back to school after lunch, so these have to be quiet and do whatever is prepared for them. It makes them very independent and they help each other.

We have a summer school for over-eight-year-olds and they go to Mount Pleasant Airport, on fishing boats, to the market garden, the swimming pool, and stay in the Stanley hostel for about ten days. We also try and encourage Stanley children to come into the Camp because they often don't know what life is like here.

Margaret and I are both members of the Bahai faith and there are about fourteen of us here now, but there's no way I would teach it in the school because a lot of parents wouldn't like it. I teach morals and get the children to think about what they're saying and doing, how to address a person when they come in, how to answer a telephone as they haven't got one yet. I call these practical life skills.

You have to be able to work independently here but I like the relaxed attitude – you're part of a society but not dependent on it. It's a good place for kids – there's no fear they would get run over or walked off with, but we do have five fenced-off mined areas here. We always ask children what they are never to do when they come to one of these fences. 'Even if you throw a ball in there, what do you do?' we ask them. The answer is 'Leave it', and they understand.

The Knitters and Shopkeepers

Eddie Chandler came out from Bath on a three-year farming contract; his wife Ann is a Falkland Islander. They now run South Atlantic Knitwear and the settlement store.

EDDIE: I first came to the Falklands because I thought it was just something different. I worked as an ordinary rouseabout, which is doing a bit of shepherding and general settlement work, until I became a full-time shepherd on a horse. When Ann and I first got married we lived in an 'outside house' eight to ten miles away from the settlement – these houses were where shepherds used to live when they were working way out on their own. We were at Teal River for eight years – it was a beautiful place.

Our son Lee was born there and when he was four we decided he needed a teacher. The policy at that time was that a single child in an outside house wasn't eligible to have one, so I ended up getting in touch with a teacher at the Darwin boarding school. He said, 'Why don't you go teaching yourself? You've got nothing to lose and I'll back you up.' I had a trial period and then took over the school at Hill Cove.

I love children and seemed to get on OK. We had as many as nine, which was quite a big class for a settlement. They were mixed ages; the oldest was fifteen and she used to teach me!

Ann and I felt we wanted some way to supplement our wages, and one of the military instructors told us that the lads were always after something with the Falklands name on it. So Ann started knitting bobble hats and she couldn't keep up, there were so many orders. The instructor said why didn't we get a knitting machine and make hats and sweaters. We did and it went on from there. There was such a good market, it seemed to me I should dig in and help. Falkland wool is beautifully soft and springy and it's nice the way it doesn't itch. We don't use any artificial dyes in getting the colours we use, like black, pebble, sandgrass, teaberry, fern and philomel blue. We sell to the Falkland Farmers Co-operative and The Pink Shop in Stanley.

We also bought Port Howard store which sells mostly food and household cleaners. It's open one afternoon a week and we never close until everyone has arrived. Port Howard is one of the nicest places to live. There's a very friendly togetherness atmosphere and it's the only farm on West Falkland that hasn't been cut into small farms, so I think everyone feels we're almost a family. There are about thirty to thirty-five people here at the moment, bu¹ three are leaving at the end of the month. I think it' because of the low wages that are dictated by the Genera Employees Union. A shepherd would be on about £320 ¹ month.

ANN: Lee is away at school in Stanley now and we go t¹ see him when we can, but it's £60 for the flight so it's no often. I think it's good for children to go away but the¹ should be able to come home more often. But if Lee passe¹ his GCSE and gets a scholarship, he's going to be awa¹ doing A levels in the UK for two years and really that's it But I suppose if you want to live here, you have to put u¹ with that sort of thing.

The Shepherd Boss

Les Morrison's father came from Scotland to work on a farm in Chartres, and his mother was born in the Falklands. He is a motorbike shepherd on Port Howard Farm settlement and is married to Lena.

LES: We've got 44,600 sheep at the moment and fou¹ shepherds, and you couldn't do shepherding on horsebac¹ here with the labour shortage of shepherds.

On a motorbike you go the same speed as the sheep a lo¹ of the time but you get there faster and you get hom¹ faster. You can now go to the furthest-away place to gathe¹ the sheep and get back home the same day. On a hors¹ we'd just be taking a day to get there. It was hard on th¹ dogs too – we could do as much as 20 miles a day. It's sti¹ quite hard but at least they have the Land Rover to com¹ home in when the day's over.

Being employed by the farm we get a free house, fre¹ milk, meat and peat too. I wouldn't mind having my ow¹ farm but don't think I ever would now because the way w¹ are, we don't have any worries. It would be good for ¹ younger man, I think.

There's always something going on: shearing starts i¹ November, in March we begin taking stock and in th¹ winter months you just work round the settlement. Fo¹ holidays we sometimes go to Stanley but don't think muc¹ of it. I'm very keen on dogs [he is a champion dog handle¹ and used to ride horses a lot. I've not been out of th¹ Falklands, but I'd like to go to England one day.

LENA: I've always lived in Camp – there are too man¹ houses in Stanley for my liking. I've only ever gone ther¹ for medicals. It just seems a big place. I get clothes by ma¹ order from Britain but sometimes from Stanley.

The Farmers

Jimmy Forster, 42, a former steelworker from Manchester, answered an advertisement for horseback shepherds in the Falklands and came down on a three-year contract in 1967. He married Ginny, 37, a Falkland Islander, and they now have three daughters and run Bold Cove Farm, an isolated 13,000-acre farm, half an hour's drive across rough moorland from Port Howard.

JIMMY: When I first came out, I lived in a bunkhouse for single men at Hill Cove. All the meals were provided but you had to bring in five bags of potatoes whether you grew them or bought them. There were no worries at all.

I lived there for eleven years and really enjoyed it. They were a very conscientious bunch of lads and you learnt the right way to do things. The only reason I left was because I heard an advert on the wireless. They were wanting a stockman as a section manager at Dunnose Head and I thought I was capable of taking that on.

When my second contract came to an end, I'd met Ginny and wanted her to go to the UK just to see if she'd like to live there. Well, Tim Blake, the manager, made me an offer that was quite something. He offered to keep me a house for twelve months as long as I would give some consideration to coming back. So we went to the UK and it was terrible. I'd been away for six or seven years by then and things do change. I didn't quite know how to say to Ginny that I'd like to go back to the Falklands, until one day I just happened to say, 'I wonder what they're doing back in the Islands?' and she said, 'Oh, wouldn't it be nice to go and find out.' So that was it. I wrote off to Tim Blake and he sent me two tickets to the Islands straight away.

A few years later when the farms were being split up, I decided I could manage one myself and in 1983 bought Packes Farm at Port Howard with 3,000 sheep. We now have 5,000 and produce about 19 tons of wool a year.

The two oldest girls, Amanda [13] and Lynne [12], go to school in Stanley and we miss them tremendously. They were very homesick at first, though we'd told them what to expect. You don't really appreciate how much they helped around the farm until they've gone.

The telephone came in last week and I've now got a computer too. The Falkland Islands Development Corporation said they'd give grants to people wanting to buy them specifically for account and stock work so they were compatible with theirs. I've also bought a peat-cutting machine with my neighbour that works off the back of a tractor. It would take me fifteen days to cut all the peat I need for the year by hand, whereas with this machine I could probably do it in two.

GINNY: You might think it would be lonely here, but it isn't. The settlement is like one big happy family, and

before we got the new telephone system, even if you
nearest neighbours were miles away, you probably knew
what they were having for dinner. We'd just shout fo
anything we wanted down the two-metre radio telephone
but you couldn't have any secrets as everyone listened in
I think it will be a lot quieter for some people now and fee
sorry for those who are away on their own. Something car
happen and they're not going to know anything about i
for weeks after.

We all help with everything that needs to be done -
sorting out the sheep, cutting peat, carrying the wool
milking the cows. When the children are home they fee
the hens and baby ducks, help in the shearing sheds an
chase the sheep into the pens. I don't know what they'll d
later on. Jimmy came a thousand miles from his home an
they're just as likely to go the opposite way, aren't they

I think we're very lucky here because we live next to
big settlement. We're on our own to do things but we'r
close enough to mix in with people, so it's great. The
storekeeper in Port Howard is very good. If we wan
something we just call up and he'll go to the store for u
and we just nip around to get it. They don't stock man
clothes, you get them mainly from mail-order catalogue
from Britain, and now that Amanda and Lynne are a
school in Stanley, they do the shopping for us. Normally
we go into Port Howard once a week and all our letters ar
delivered there. It's a real social centre - you often get
party that can last for hours! It doesn't take us long to ge
there, but if you do twelve miles an hour by car in th
Falklands, you're doing well. The tracks get pretty mudd
and sometimes the car gets bogged down and you have t
walk home, so you just go back in the morning with
tractor to get it.

The Dairy Manager

*Pauline McCormick,
Manager of Mount Maria
Dairy, came to the Falklands
from Hampshire with her
parents in 1957 when she was
7 years old. Her father was
the Port Howard accountant,
storekeeper and gardener. She
went to school in the UK,
returned to the Falklands,
married when she was 16, and
has four children. Her
husband died in 1986.*

My daughter works in the UK and wouldn't come back for the world. One son is doing an apprenticeship as a carpenter in Stanley, one is a contract shearer who travels around and makes a lot of money, and one is still at school. I do think, although I love the Falklands, they don't have a lot to offer that age group. Maybe they've got to see the bright lights to realise what they've got here.

The Falkland Islanders are lovely people and very responsible. You don't get any abandoned mothers or babies here, and the trend is to live together. They may be a bit slow on the uptake sometimes but that's because of the peaceful way they live. They don't have too much hassle. There's no unemployment but no dole either.

I have fifty-three dairy cows which are rather inbred so not a very good herd but we're hoping to build them up, and I supply the settlement with two gallons of milk per household a day – that's about twelve or fourteen houses. Any surplus I get I separate and make into cream and butter and sell to Stanley. Before I got a grant from the Falkland Islands Development Corporation to set up the dairy, it was owned by Port Howard Farm and they employed me to run it. Every Falkland Islands girl learns how to make butter and cream when she's about ten.

I suppose a typical day would start at four o'clock. I do the Tourist Lodge fires and get to the cows at about quarter to five. It takes me two and a half hours to milk them with the rather antique machines we have. I come back to the Lodge, scrub up and am waitress for breakfast. Then there's bread and cakes to be made, dishes to be washed. We don't have a person for one specific job – we all help each other. The cook washes dishes and the cleaner sometimes cooks. In the afternoon I milk the cows again and prepare for the evening meal. My day ends about 9.30. I think my tired time comes after lunch. I'd like to sleep then for an hour or so if I could.

An Old Shepherd

George Llamosa, shepherd, died when he was about 90 in the early 1970s. Three people who knew him well talk about their memories of him.

Mike Summers, General Manager of the Falkland Islands Development Corporation: Uncle George was my great-uncle. He went out as a boy to Purvis – that's one of the shepherds' houses about 16 miles from Port Howard. I believe he might have been only fourteen or fifteen years old when he started, and he basically spent the whole of his life shepherding there. You hardly ever saw him in Port Howard. People took his stores out to him.

I only ever remember him as an old man – reasonably tall, slightly bent. He had this wonderful way of talking which amused us all – a very slow, deliberate voice, slightly quavering.

I remember the visits to Purvis as a kid. Uncle George was always there, standing on the step waiting to greet us. He was a fabulous cook and made huge amounts of food. He was always so pleased to see people, but by about four o'clock in the afternoon he'd look at his watch and say, 'Well, I suppose you chaps will need to be going soon.' One day was enough for him.

But there were times when, as youngsters, we would go out and stay for one or two days, and he loved that because as long as there weren't too many people about he was happy. He'd sit down and play crib with us and spin yarns about old chaps and the things he'd done.

What people often remember about Uncle George is the number of pairs of slippers he used to keep so that everyone who went there could have a pair to wander about the house in. He kept them all on the table – I suppose they were his old ones.

He had, I'd guess, about 5,000 or 6,000 sheep to look after, and every evening at eight o'clock the boss used to lift the telephone for all the shepherds to report what was going on and receive their orders for the next day. If a shepherd failed to pick up the phone, the boss would be concerned, and if he didn't pick it up the following day he'd go and see what the problem was.

Brook Hardcastle, former Manager of the Falkland Island Company farms on East Falkland: George was a slim, dapper and bald-headed little chap and would do anything for anybody. He taught me so much and he'd give you anything. We all made our own horse gear, and he'd explain how to do it and how to cook a cow's udder, which is beautiful to eat. He'd shoot coranchos, too, and cook them. These were one of the few wild birds with a gizzard and I thought they couldn't be nice to eat, they're pretty lanky-looking birds. But we shot a couple of them, did them up and you wouldn't have known them from chicken. They were beautiful. He'd cook currant bread, milk loaves, you name it, and he'd cook it on his old Stanley range.

He was a very unassuming man but he could be very cruel. I saw him chop a dog's head off with a spade just because it annoyed him.

Robin Lee, joint-owner with his brother of Port Howard Farm and General Manager of Falklands Landholdings Ltd: As far as I know George Llamosa never went to Stanley in forty years, but he used to have the *Daily Mirror* sent out to him in book form and kept right up to date with what was going on.

Visitors never understood how they were always offered freshly made currant buns when George didn't know they were coming. And then someone discovered he made them every day for his dog. I think he was about ninety when he died and hadn't been back to the Port Howard settlement for four or five years.

He lived by the shore and used to throw his mutton bones straight into the sea from his back door. When he was too old to get a sheep up to his house, he'd tie it to a horse to be dragged there. He'd have potatoes a month before anyone else, and carrots one and a half times as long, and he'd make his own horse gear from rawhide. When people get married in the Falklands everyone writes recipes down for them in an exercise book, and George gave my mother his Bachelors' Breakfast: goose eggs, fritters, cold meat with onion and batter.

He retired when he was about seventy but worked on for another fifteen years. One night, he told me later, he thought he was going to die, gave all his bread to his hens because he felt it would be some days before anyone found him, lay down and crossed his arms so it would be easy to put him into a coffin.

Some months later he *was* taken ill and I went over to his cabin. He said to me, 'I'm not going to come back.' He knew he was going to die. He walked down to the shore, got into a boat to take him to hospital and looked back a few times. He didn't show any emotion, but he knew. I was left alone in the house he'd been in for fifty years and I knew too that he wouldn't come back.

Darwin and Goose Green

These two settlements are on the narrow isthmus that separates Lafonia in the south from the rest of East Falkland. Goose Green, 60 miles from Stanley, was established in 1875 as the site of a tallow factory. By the end of the century only thirteen people were living there but by the 1920s the population had increased to 185. The wool shed, built in 1927, and big enough for 5,000 sheep is said to be the largest in the world. There was a 40-bed boarding school here for Camp children until the late 1970s when it was decided that secondary-school children should go to school in Stanley. The school was burnt down in the war and a new one for younger children has been built. Seventeen British soldiers lost their lives here during the war; 235 Argentinians are buried in a small cemetery on the hillside.

Thirty-seven people live here now, farming the 430,000 acres. Nutt Cartnel, who lives in a cottage with giant yellow pansies in the small fenced garden, is reputed to have an unrivalled Falkland Islands stamp collection, but didn't want to talk about stamps. So we spoke of other things like mending fences, which is his job when he's not helping out with the sheep at shearing time. He gets order from France to supply seeds and has a lively trade in Land Rover spare parts, videos and T-shirts.

Darwin took its name from Charles Darwin, who is said to have spent a night here in 1833. The settlement started some twenty-five years later when the vicar's house was built. The farm manager's house today is close to the shore with lovely views of Mount Usborne, which at 2,312 feet is the highest mountain in the Falklands.

The Retired Farm Manager

At 19, Brook Hardcastle answered an advertisement for a shepherd in the Falklands and was engaged as an apprentice on a five-year contract. Apart from ten years in New Zealand, he has been in the Falklands ever since and has now, forty years later, just retired as General Manager of the Falkland Islands Company farms at Goose Green, North Arm, Walker Creek and Fitzroy on East Falkland. He is married to Eileen, a Falkland Islander and former travelling teacher. They live at Darwin on East Falkland and have three grown-up children.

I used to get up at five o'clock in the morning, have an hour's dig in the vegetable garden, fill up the stove, bring the vegetables in, saw up the meat and make sure everything was hunky-dory for the meals of the day. Officially I started work at six, did office work or went to Goose Green [a mile away]. It takes six months to get anything sent out here from the UK and you have to be sure you have enough flour, all the hoops and bagging, and enough spare parts for the shearing motors. Then I had the budgeting to do, the government-grant schemes to make out, make sure there was enough fuel in the generator, enough potatoes in the house and that the chickens were laying. I also had people throwing stones at my window at 3.30 in the morning, saying, 'Will you come and sort out Fred because he's just punched me up.' That was Diamond Lil, as we call her, and she said, 'Thank you very effing much,' when I said I wasn't coming to sort out her husband! I am a JP and can do anything, bury you if you like, sign passports, it's all paternalism. Of course I enjoyed it or I wouldn't be here, but I couldn't have managed without Eileen. You had to be on the ball twenty-five hours a day, know everyone's weaknesses and strengths, and there were a few surprises when we were locked up in the hall in the Conflict. Those you thought might be leaders just lay there like dead people.

At the beginning of the Conflict, a Captain Gomez, whose wife, we later discovered, went to school with our daughter, came to find me and read out this edict: 'We've come to free you from colonialism. We shall protect you. There's nothing to worry about. You carry on your life as usual. But we want that Land Rover and that Land Rover, and where are we going to live?' We eventually evacuated the boarding school for their headquarters.

On May 1 we heard on the six o'clock news that the British had bombed the airport. The next morning there were twelve [Argentinian] anti-insurgency aeroplanes on our airstrip, and very heavily armed they were. We were thinking, why didn't the British knock hell out of them, and no sooner had we said that, than three Harriers flew over the airport and blew them all up. Things became very difficult then because they killed quite a lot of people, eleven were buried up here by the racecourse. The Argentines rounded us all up [115 people] and put us in

the recreation hall under the pretext that it was for our
own protection. Eileen and I were there for sixteen days
but many others were there for thirty.

There were only two loos, nothing to eat, no beds. The
only thing we had was a bar, so we weren't short of booze
for a while. There were thirty-five people under fifteen, the
youngest three months old, three over eighty, and twenty
had come from Stanley thinking they'd be safe here but
they'd gone out of the frying pan into the fire. Every time
we opened the door, there were eight guards outside who
cocked their rifles and said, 'Shut the door,' and that was
that. Eventually they allowed me to go to the store. It was
difficult to see in the dark but I got cream crackers, ham,
baked beans, tomatoes and toilet paper. When you have to
get things for 115 people you wonder what's the most
important. That was all we had for three days and then two
officers came in and we started talking, but everything was
mañana, there was no hurry. It didn't matter to them that
we had no change of clothes, or water was difficult.

Things got better. Val Ellis, the cook, was allowed to go
and bake bread, but of course the damned Aga was out and
it took five hours to get it going. Two shepherds were
allowed out to round up ten sheep, which they killed and
hung them in the meat house, but when we went back in the
morning they'd gone because the Argentines had pinched
them. I told them they were treating us worse than the
Japanese and Germans treated people. I said, 'You wait
you'll get your comeuppance.' And they said, 'No, signor
you're here for your own protection.' In fact when they
eventually let us out, a lot of people felt safer in a crowd and
wouldn't go home, though some couldn't because their
houses had been taken over.

During the battle, the British lost seventeen people here
including Colonel H. Jones. Colonels don't get killed but
he did. The Argentines lost fifty-four and there were
several killed afterwards because they'd booby-trapped the
trenches. What a hell of a thing to do.

On the night of the 28th, the warships from San Carlos
seventeen miles away were shelling us with airbursts to
keep the Argentines' heads down while the four companie
of paratroopers were getting themselves into their star
positions. The battle started at eight o'clock and went on
and on. I can understand why people get shell-shocked. I

finished at two o'clock, just like that. It was so quiet you couldn't believe it and then, a minute or two later, the whole place lit up just as though it was daylight. They'd fired these pyrotechnics and in the yellow light you could see the drifting-down parachutes, but everything was a kind of double image. There was a soldier running across the green and it looked like two, like a negative. At five o'clock we thought the house was on fire, a 105 shell landed 20 metres away and, oh crikey, we just didn't know what was going to happen. The battle went on all that day.

There's an enormous potential for development in Lafonia [the southern area of East Falkland] but I can't get any sense out of the Agricultural Research Centre people. You have to run more sheep to grow more wool to pay for the inflation, and the only way to run more sheep is to grow more grass. And doing that costs a lot of risk money because if you have £1,000 and put it into grassland, you don't get anything back for two years at least, and all the seed might blow away and might not grow. But if you had the £1,000 and took it to the Halifax Building Society you'd get $x\%$ tomorrow. It's very difficult to convince these people here. When you look into their eyes they have a pound sign in one and a dollar in the other. But the money's there and to me it's so obvious what we have to do.

I don't think the money from the fishing industry is being well spent. Absolutely not. It seems to us who live in Camp that all the money has so far been spent in Stanley. New hospital, swimming pool, senior school. That's dead money to me. We in Camp pay taxes the same as anyone else, though we can't take advantage of the amenities in Stanley. Too much has been spent on dead infrastructure and almost a negligible percentage on revenue-producing projects. If only they'd put out a little more risk money to grow grass for sheep, start a mushroom farm, or anything that in the long term would produce revenue to keep the thing going.

The Craftswoman

Eileen Hardcastle is a fourth-generation Islander. Her father, a shepherd, later took over the Stanley Arms pub in Stanley. A former travelling teacher, she now spins wool, makes and sells rugs and provides accommodation and meals for visitors.

I started spinning in my school days and when we got married I bought a wheel. Brook said, 'Oh, I think I can do this,' and he started doing it too. It's very companionable. Every evening we change and come into the spinning room and listen to the local news and at six o'clock turn over to London.

I've been trying to do rugs for years with various methods, but this is the most successful. I wash the raw skin, soak it in salt and then scrape off the little bits of meat and fat, soak it in soda and salt for twenty-four hours, wash it again, then paint it with a chemical three or four times over two days. This turns the skin blue, but that washes out. Then I stretch the skin over an old wooden ironing board, wash it in Lux flakes and paint it with vegetable oil. Brook does the trimming and the last part is the brushing. I've made about fifty so far and sell them in Stanley and Mount Pleasant.

We make toast racks, egg spoons and cups, and serviette rings out of cows' horns. But you can't just go and get the horn of a newly dead cow, you have to wait for it to weather. I also plait cows' tails, which I hang on the wall by a mirror to put combs in. We've used Argentine ammunition boxes for our antirrhinums and a bullet for an ashtray.

I find it difficult when I go shopping in the UK, though I do stock up on clothes when I go, which is every two and a half years, for I have everything to hand here and just use what I've got. I usually bake a sponge cake before breakfast, and if I have bread to make I like to do it then too, because there are lots of interruptions afterwards. I think life is more exciting since the Conflict but it has never been quiet.

When the first-time members of the Falkland Families came here I could hardly face them. I felt that they were all here because they had lost loved ones trying to save us. We have talked about it since and it has become easier.

The Farm Cook

Val Ellis came from the Isles of Scilly when she and her husband heard that a cook was needed at the Falkland Islands Company farm settlement at Goose Green.

I was a bit apprehensive about cooking for the shearers because I didn't know what food they would like. It was rather like the Wild West then, well it is now really, but the lady who was cook at the time showed me and we got on famously. Shearers are the fastest eaters in the world. This morning at breakfast there were about eleven of them and ten shepherds, and they had as many chops as they wanted, two fried eggs each, fritters and spaghetti, toast and fried bread, and then came over for about another loaf and a half to make more toast.

We go fishing quite often and bring back mullet, smelt and beautiful sea trout from the shore. I don't know any of the techniques, I just throw a hook and pull them out. We use penguin, goose and duck eggs, and when the goslings are what I call teenagers, their legs are cut off and cooked in breadcrumbs. Except for empanadas and cazuela [chicken or goose stew], all the cooking is English or Scottish. Of course you have to make everything you want, and you can't get an egg unless you have a hen. I've learnt how to pickle beef and mutton in brine, and pickle eggs in water-glass to keep when the hens go off laying in winter.

We have beef all winter time because there's more shepherds to go out chasing wild animals. They shoot them and bring them home on a sleigh but sometimes they lasso them. The only time you cook in advance is for Sports Week because we don't know how many people will come. Some families have as many as twenty to thirty staying with them, and they put the men in one room and the women in another. There are usually sheep-dog trials on the first day, which are very boring because they're based on the UK system. I don't think they should be, because we're not the UK. You get these dogs that are used to 5,000 sheep suddenly presented with just five, and you can see that instead of listening to the whistle they're looking for the rest. There's horse-racing, egg and spoon and sack races, steer riding, which is the big thing, and a veterans' race for everyone over forty. If you're like Sandy Coots, who is nearly eighty, your nose is practically touching the winning post before you start.

I think it's the personal freedom that I like so much about living here. You can go where you want to, do what you want. I'm not very sociable and they do respect your privacy, but if you feel like mixing there's darts in the winter and dances, and if you do want to talk, you've only got to go round and open the door and there's probably four or five people there — they haven't lost the art of conversation here yet.

We're building a house in Stanley, putting our roots down and hoping to be a Bennie one day. In the TV programme *Crossroads* there was some dimwit who always wore a woolly hat, called Bennie, and when the troops came down here I expect they saw Islanders with woolly hats and assumed they would be as thick as Bennie was. But we were talking to a military person one day and he said to me, 'You're going to join the Cheys, are you?' which is what Islanders call each other, and I thought that was quite nice.

Fox Bay East

Fox Bay East was bought by the Government from Packe Brothers in 1983 and is now the only village in the Falklands. It has an elected council with five members, and elections are held every year. Every three months there's a general meeting with everyone, as one Councillor said, having a good old shout.

About thirty to forty people live here in their own or rented houses, which are scattered round a large grassy area. There's a school with three children, a shop, a hundred-year-old post office and a mill that spins yarn for hand and machine knitting in soft Falkland colours. The settlement is a refuelling base for RAF helicopters, and has a commercial knitwear business and a salmon-farming project, while Reg Anderson produces enough vegetables in his garden to supply local people and hotels in Stanley.

The social club meets every other Saturday in a hall decorated with trophies and a Union Jack. There is a snooker table at one end and a bar at the other, and wives take it in turns to cook Village Suppers, with mutton sausages, mashed potatoes and peas, and creamy-topped sponge cakes. On Sunday morning there's a Glory Hour with darts and snooker.

Fox Bay West across the bay, once as large as Fox Bay East, now has only three families and no shop. The track between the two settlements is so bad it's often impassable in winter months.

The Entrepreneur

Richard Cockwell came to the Falklands in 1964, when he was 25 years old, as an assistant farm manager. He married Grizelda on a visit to Britain and they have three sons. When the farms were sold for subdivision in 1983, they started a woollen mill in Fox Bay, of which Richard became Chairman.

My grandparents were farmers and I wanted to be a shepherd since I was three years old. I became one when I left school, and worked on Salisbury Plain. At seventeen I went to live on a sheep farm in Australia for three years until the job of an assistant farm manager in the Falklands came up, and later I took over as manager of three farms with 150,000 acres and 33,000 sheep. It was farming on a grand scale with these wide-open spaces and really suited me. There were about thirty people living at Fox Bay then.

Life was very different in those days. You hear about the feudal system of the Falklands but I think maternalistic is a better word. My social life was very structured, and when we went to Stanley for farmers' meetings it was made perfectly clear that one's social events and cocktail parties were organised for you, and you never got a chance to meet anyone outside that sort of circle.

You couldn't telephone the UK in those days. You had a single-wire system right round West Falkland with switches that would go from one manager's house to the next, and we used that. There was a wireless station at Fox Bay which could send messages by Morse code to Stanley, so it was an almost confidential link. And there were the black boxes that hummed and whistled when we tried to send messages. Mail from overseas came once a month by ship and was sorted out in Stanley and put on to the planes that went round dropping bags from the air.

When Packes Farm, where I worked, was sold in 1983, Griz and I had to decide whether we wanted to carry on farming or do something else. We'd been saying for years it was time someone started something new in the Falklands. I'd been interested in wool processing and we looked at the idea of setting up a mill. The Government said the British Council would pay for my training and we got swept along with the idea, which got bigger than we first envisaged. Fox Bay Mill was to be the first place wool could be processed in the Falklands.

There followed a series of disasters: two tons of machinery got lost and turned up six months later in Pakistan, and technicians sent down from the Scottish College of Textiles to put the machines together couldn't wait for them to arrive. In 1985 Richard, although remaining as Chairman, decided to do something else and became involved in road-improvement projects.

Our three children were born here and they've coped

with the cultural change of being at school in Stanley pretty well. Having the new phone has made a big difference. Before that it was very difficult to talk to them, as they hated the RT [radio telephone]. You do miss them but you have to let them go and make up their own minds whether they want to stay in the Falklands.

It was very difficult during the war because the Argentines hardly spoke any English and the Islanders any Spanish. We had enough Spanish to get by, and one day I went to the Commander and said some people wanted to go and live with their families elsewhere. He said they could, but what he didn't realise was that everyone was going except Grizelda and I and one shepherd. People in Stanley were fortunate because except for a small number, they didn't have to deal with the Argentinians first hand. But here, if anything went wrong, it was our fault. We'd be sitting in the kitchen like this and all of a sudden the door would burst open and they'd be in. I was so angry all the time I wasn't really aware of the strain. At the surrender they said they'd cleared up all the mines, but they hadn't and they're still here. The worst place in the whole of the Falklands is Fox Bay West. There have been more accidents there than the rest of the Falklands put together. The Argentine second-in-command, who was a decent bloke, said to me, 'If I was you, I would never go to Fox Bay West again for the rest of my days.' The way they've laid the mines over there is nothing but criminal. They don't know where they are and no one else will ever know.

The war has left a scar on some people more than others. We didn't talk about it for a long time at all. I think some felt guilty they'd left us, and we certainly didn't want to make a big issue of it. In some ways, although it was more lonely, it was easier after they had gone. We couldn't have gone on escorting everyone to their hen runs and out to their cowsheds as we'd had to do. It was surprising how much better my Spanish got. I expect if I got angry it would come out again.

It's got to be in the back of one's mind that there could be a lease-back arrangement but there's no point worrying about something you can't do anything about. I think you've got to make it evident to everyone that there *are* people committed to living in the Falklands, and this is their home and this is where they are going to stay. We just haven't got the political muscle to be independent.

The Knitwear Designer

Grizelda Cockwell taught at Fox Bay School, worked at the mill and now runs her own company, Warrah Knitwear, designing and knitting sweaters and scarves.

During the war, the settlement was empty because everyone left except us and one shepherd called George. Up until the Conflict I had never had much to do with George because he was excessively shy. Whenever he used to come and see Richard he'd knock at the back door and look down and say, 'Good day, Mrs Cockwell, is the boss in?' and I'd say, 'Yes, George, do you want to come in?' and he'd say, 'No, just want to see the boss.' And that was that. I never spoke any other word to him that I can recall. Then on the day in the Conflict when everyone wanted to leave and Richard and I were feeling a bit down in the dumps, more apprehensive than frightened, George came to the door and said, 'Good day, Mrs Cockwell, I believe you people are staying here.' And I said, 'Yes, that's right.' And he said, 'Well, I don't think it's right that you should be on your own and if you'll give me lodgings I'll stay with you.' I would have hugged him if I hadn't thought it would have frightened him off. And so he came in and lived with us for about eighteen months. He was just a member of the family and a wonderful chap. He died about seven years ago and I really miss him.

To live in the Falklands, you have to be the sort of person who can rub along tolerably easily with other people. If your marriage is a bit rocky, it will be difficult, because you're thrown on your own resources all the time. You know how it is in a good marriage, you depend on each other and have a lot of interaction. But because you're thrown together so much, there only have to be small cracks in this dependence and they get bigger. You haven't got the distractions. In larger communities you can have a blazing row and I could say, 'I'm going to go back and stay with my mum for a few days, to hell with you.' But you can't do that here. And Richard can't fling himself out of the house and say he's going down to the pub for a few hours. You can go for a walk or kick a penguin, but you haven't got those safety valves. Some people are quite happy to be discontented with their lot, and wherever they go, they'll trail a big black cloud around with them. We see it happening any number of times here. People who are dissatisfied with their lives in Britain say, 'Right, we're going to up sticks and move somewhere else.' But they carry their own problems along the line. If you're the kind of person who can recognise where problems may be and

adapt and still be content, that's probably the qualities you most need here.

But there are not many other places in the world where you could have your four-year-old saying 'Mum, can you make me a sandwich, because I want to go off on my bike for a picnic?' and he cycles away over the horizon out of sight and you just don't worry, no harm can come to him.

SAM COCKWELL, 4: Everyone here is my friend.

The Schoolteacher

Niamh Howlett worked in cancer research in London before her husband was sent to the Falklands with the Agricultural Research Council. She now runs the school in Fox Bay East, which has three children.

I was assistant to one of the travelling teachers first, then took over full-time. It's not difficult, you just have to start with the basics. There's Angela, who's nine, Anika, seven, and Sam Cockwell, who's four and has been coming on Friday mornings to break him in gently. I also have three children from Fox Bay West coming over for two days a week, and five radio lessons, so I'm quite busy.

It's hard to teach young children on the radio. There's one boy who is just six and nowhere near reading or writing. I've been told to expand his vocabulary, get him talking about different things and teach him to count. The travelling teacher teaches him to read and write.

Although the children go into Stanley quite often, I have to explain things like motorways and skyscrapers and traffic lights. But they pick things up fairly quickly. They are very good on Island wildlife and have taught me a lot about that. I have no discipline problems at all. I hope to be more of a friend to the children than a teacher, because I see them when I go to the store and the social club, and they come down here to my house just to say hello. Parents don't come into the school. I think the standard of education for them wasn't very good and they tend to stay away, but everyone is on first-name terms. There's only twenty of us and I never feel lonely. If someone wants to come and see me, they just come. They don't ring up and say, 'I'll be over at 3.30.' That's unheard of.

The Village Agent

Ken Halliday deals with government business concerning Fox Bay, maintains the generators, keeps the village accounts, collects rents, reads electricity meters and meets incoming aircraft. He is also Deputy Postmaster and Secretary of the Southern Cross Social Club.

I just work as I feel like it but that can be any time from six o'clock in the morning to ten o'clock at night. If something crops up, say we have a problem with the water which we can't cope with — it comes from the spring, and the demand is often greater than the supply when it hasn't rained for some time — then the Government will send someone out to look at it, and I deal with him. I've married people (in the post office) and only had one failure, but had a second go at that one! If I want to have a break, say go out and do a bit of fishing, I take the afternoon off. I like fishing but there aren't a great many other hobbies you can do here. I visit a lot of people on various farms, just to say hello, and that gets you away from the place for a little while. When Fox Bay West was fully intact [see p.101], I'd go there for a change and have a party round that side. Now the farm is broken up and a lot of people are outside the settlement, it's a bit of a hassle for them to come in at weekends. That's the only thing I find with the splitting-up of the farms — it's dampened the community spirit. We built our house ourselves, but most of the other houses here are government owned and people pay rent. It's very little, £60 odd a month, and they're mainly for mill workers.

Money gets paid into the social club, the club pays it into the store, and the store pays it out as change. We had a naval ship in here once, they went to the club and spent quite a bit of money — that was great, we had a batch of new notes and were well off for money again. If we want to watch television, we send five tapes to a friend in Stanley who records programmes for us, and once we've seen them we parcel them up and send them back for the next batch.

Our son Geoffrey is fifteen, and we'll probably see him about two or three times a year because he's working all round the farms. Once you're fifteen you can be employed for a small period of time during the day. I think it's a maximum of eight hours.

It would be good to see the mill making a profit. The last manager left under a cloud but the major problem was that the Falkland Islands Development Corporation bought a load of antiquated equipment. I'd also like money spent on all-weather track, something people could drive on in the middle of the winter and be able to say, 'I'll go and see so-and-so in Port Stevens [about 50 miles away] and be back for supper,' which you can't do now. I'm not talking about three-lane traffic, but something just wide enough for a Land Rover or car to pass, even a single lane, if you like. At present, if you go three or four miles away from here, you have tracks made by a bulldozer that has bulldozed all the surface off, and they're down to solid clay. All we need are a few potholes filled up and levelled off and maybe two ditches dug down each side for the water to drain away. We could then have someone to maintain it at a minute cost. The trouble with the Government is that roads have to be made to certain specifications, so they call down these experts whom they have to listen to, and tracks that have lasted for the last thirty years are probably no good as far as they're concerned.

Pebble Island

In 1846 an Englishman, John Henry Dean, bought four islands in the Falklands for £400 and started a sheep-farming company that still exists today. One of the islands was called Pebble and this can now be reached on a forty-minute flight from Stanley. It is 22 miles long, covers 21,000 acres and is controlled by the UK-based Dean Brothers Ltd, but managed locally by Raymond Evans, whose father's Great-Uncle Johnny was involved with the slaughter of the first wild cattle and the introduction of sheep here.

The island, which was one of the first settlements to harness wind power to generate electricity, now has 13,500 Corriedale sheep and some 240 head of beef and dairy cattle. Wild duck, grebe and black-necked swans live on the freshwater ponds, and colonies of seals can be seen on the rocky coasts along with gentoo, magellanic and rockhopper penguins.

About fourteen men, women and children live here with one store, a one-classroom school and a hotel with six twin rooms complete with en suite bathrooms. The island's grass airstrip was used by the Argentines when they landed several hundred troops on Pebble and based a number of aircraft here. These were later destroyed by the SAS and it was after that raid that the Islanders were imprisoned and spent the rest of the war in the manager's house. A memorial cross on First Mountain commemorates the casualties from *HMS Coventry*, which sank fourteen miles off Pebble Island in May 1982.

The Assistant Farm Manager's Wife

Sue Hirtle, 41, was born and brought up at Port Howard. She has three children by a previous marriage.

I open the settlement shop three nights a week and if the shearers are here and there's a big crowd, it's every night. But if anyone's desperate for anything I open it anyway. I just keep the basic things there because you have a very limited turnover, though the hotel makes a big difference. A lot of the stuff we get from Stanley is just about out of date, but I don't think it matters too much. If a tin has a tiny dent in it, I'll say to someone, 'Go home and try it out and if it's not right, I'll refund the money.' You can't be as particular as you are in England or you'd end up with nothing.

You do have to look ahead a bit and if you strike a problem no one is going to have much sympathy for you. It's silly things really. I ordered toothbrushes for over a year before I got them. And I just couldn't get Rennies indigestion tablets that two or three people wanted, and I'm sure they thought I wasn't really trying.

Society is changing very quickly in the Falklands and there are very few big farm settlements left. Even a few years ago there were a lot more people on Pebble. I don't think the settlements should be split up so much, because you get young people wanting to work on a farm and they have a difficult time finding a job because the new small farms are family units and can't afford to employ people.

Sammy [her youngest child, aged eight] has a teacher who comes for ten days, and then has radio lessons for half an hour each day on the two-metre radio. I do homework with her, and the rest of the day is her own. But at her age I don't think that's wrong because the teaching is very intensive on a one-to-one basis. After lessons, she just takes herself and the dogs and disappears, and I don't have to worry about who's going to pick her up and whisk her away. She does quite a bit of riding, so she goes to work with Turtle [Sue's husband, whose real name is Tony] when he's working the horses – and she hops on and off the Islander plane as though it was a bus. She thinks Andy [the pilot] is the cat's whiskers because he lets her sit in the co-pilot's seat.

So far as my day is concerned, in the summer I have to milk the cows, about twenty at present, and be out of the cowshed by six. So I sometimes start work around half-three or four in the morning. Then I get breakfast for the shearers: cereals, bread rolls, chops, beans, the works. I separate the milk and sort out the buckets (at the moment we get about 5 gallons), do the peat stoves, cart the peat in and cart the ashes out. And every time you do that you can guarantee another layer of dust. We do have good peat here – it's very crumbly. You get some that's a palish-brown and we call it book peat because if you chop or break it, it comes out in flat sheets like paper, and there's no heat in that.

We make our own butter and bread, and if you want sausage rolls, you have to cut the meat off the sheep to get it. It's not like popping down to the shop in the UK – you've got to start right from scratch, so everything takes longer. We eat quite a bit of bread – I use about 9 lb. of flour at a go. It's white bread and I've always been meaning to try brown, but you could buy white flour in 50-kilo sacks until recently at the West Store in Stanley.

Shearers don't eat so much in the middle of the day. I usually give them cold meat, salad or potatoes and a cold pudding, and they have cakes and coffee down at the shearing shed halfway through the spell. We have supper about half-past six and that's always a hot meal. We caught forty-three fish the night before last down by the jetty, but that's the first we've had for ages – we don't think the fish are around like they were a few years ago, but that's another debate.

I'm inclined to get very grouchy if I don't get out, and we ride most evenings in the summer – we have five horses which we also use for getting the cows in. It's surprising how much time your animals take up – we've all got hens, dogs and cats, and by the time you've done the round and the peat stove, the daylight seems to be running out.

I've been away from the Falklands a few times and have considered not coming back, but I always seem to and I don't think I'd change what I've got now. I was six and a half years at school and college in the UK, and I always vowed I'd never send my kids away to school because of that. I went when I was eleven and came back at seventeen. It's a long time, you grow away from your parents and I think it left me with a few hang-ups. You couldn't come home for holidays because by the time you got here via Montevideo and Stanley it was time to go back again. In fact my brother never came back. Until recently a lot of elderly people living in Camp had to retire to Stanley, and that's what happened to my parents. But they didn't want to live there and went back to the UK where my mother was born.

The Hotel Cook

Ann Prior, 42, runs a hotel on Fair Isle when she is not cooking at Pebble Island Hotel during the southern summer months.

I answered an advertisement in the *Shetland Times* for a cook in the Falklands and got the job. I always wanted to come here as I'm a very keen bird-watcher, and everyone I know would have given their eye teeth to have come too. Here on Pebble Island there are peregrines and red-backed hawks, penguins, of course, and black-necked swans. There's an excellent sea-lion colony too.

When I first arrived there was no private telephone and everyone talked on the radio telephone. I used to switch on and listen to it and the chat was brilliant, you really felt you got to know everyone. That's what makes it more sociable here than you might expect because even if you don't talk to anyone yourself, you have people chattering away in your kitchen. You know what they're doing and getting up to, and when you finally meet them you can stick a face to a name and feel quite familiar with them.

It's nice being able to use local ingredients and the meat is fantastic. Apart from meat and salad vegetables, which are grown here, we get geese and penguin eggs and I've cooked a shag egg too. It's a very translucent white with pinky-orange yolk. The shop opens three days a week and has all the basics but doesn't have perishables or a deep freeze, so we do a bulk order by phone to Stanley and this is delivered by ship.

Our water supply comes down a pipe to a storage tank, but not quickly enough, so we have to go up to a spring on First Mountain and pump the water into two 500-gallon tanks which we bring down in the tractor. I cook on a peat stove with a little electric oven at the back of the cooker to boost it.

I watch birds, sunbathe, read all the books in the house, go visiting. People don't socialise very much here because they're working together all the time, well, that's on Pebble Island anyway. They all go to bed about 8.30 pm, so by the time I've knocked off work at nine, everybody's asleep.

Young Falkland Islanders are tremendously lively, enjoy themselves and love the place. They're very resourceful and radiate well-being and independence, and the children are great fun, too, and think for themselves. What Islanders don't seem to want to do is make decisions or to change things if they can help it. When I compare them with those in the Shetlands, they're extremely undemanding.

The Handyman and Gardener

Hernan Torres, 30, was born in Chile, studied English in Punta Arenas, worked as a guide and ran a taxi service. He came to the Falklands in 1989 and his wife Elena, 32, a schoolteacher, followed a year later. They have two small children, who doubled the school population of Pebble Island.

I am the fourth member of my family to come here. The last one, my uncle, was a handyman for twenty years. The economic situation is very bad in Chile and I came here for six months to see what I would find. I liked what I saw and now work as a handyman gardener. Perhaps I am not doing what I studied for but I feel very happy. The people are very friendly, though not quite the same as those in Chile. I think they go to work very young here and forget their relations in some ways. They make their own lives. In Chile, it's not like that. You can be married like me and I go to my mother's or grandmother's house every day. They both live alone and I think we may have to go back for them. My grandmother is eighty-seven and we don't have many more years with her in life.

When Elena picks up some English she could teach Spanish in the local school, but at the moment she does the washing-up, cleaning and helps with the cooking.

The Islander

Cinty Betts spent most of her life on Pebble Island. She was sent out to work at 12 as a table maid, nursemaid and cook, and at 20 she married a shepherd and handyman. Later she lived with her son Arthur John.

I remember when you had to light fires outside if you wanted anything from another island: three fires for a doctor, two for the mail. I never liked Stanley and I wouldn't take work there even when I was single. People always have colds or something, and I haven't been there now for about three years. In the war we were all shut up in the manager's house here on Pebble Island and were in darkness. We weren't even allowed a torch. There were twenty-five of us in there, all shut up for thirty-one days, but we had good food, the manager saw to that. There were 300 Argentinians here, more than we wanted – and we were glad to see the back of them.

I say I'm the oldest person on the island and the biggest dunce, but I can't help that. I had to go out to work instead of going to school, and I didn't get paid for it either. Now we get peat given to us from the farm, as well as milk and mutton. The only thing I have to pay for is electricity, and that's because I've retired.

On Christmas Day 1990 Cinty died, while having a cup of tea in bed, at the age of 91.

Carcass Island

Carcass Island was named after the ship *HMS Carcas*
which came to the Falklands in 1776. It lies north-west o
West Falkland and is about 6 miles long and 2 miles wid
at its widest point. Rob and Lorraine McGill, who bough
the island in 1974 and farm 1,240 sheep on its 4,250 acres
are the only people to live here except for Aunt Agnes
Agnes Hoggarth, 67, a Falkland Islander, married a
Englishman and lived for eleven years in Filey, Yorkshir
before returning to the Falklands. She lives in Stanley bu
comes to help Rob with the baking for cruise-shi
passengers who visit Carcass on their way to the Antarctic

The McGills' house was built in 1938 and lies on th
edge of the shore, surrounded by trees, which are a rar
sight in the Falklands. It's an attractive, rambling, one
storey building with rooms leading off a central carpete
passage. The sitting room has books, records, Cockburn
port on the drinks shelf, photographs, a video, an
miniature shields on the walls. The large yet cosy kitche
is furnished with painted blue chests and comfortab
chairs, and has a lovely view through the trees where nigh
herons nest. In the sheltered, almost tropical garden, Ne
Zealand palm trees and fuchsias grow. Nearby are
grocery store, stables, a wool shed and a cowshed. There
also a building in which the fat from sheep carcasses w
once melted before being tipped into 40-gallon drum
sealed up and sent off to England for candle-making.

Just up the hill from the house are two weatherboarde
red-roofed cottages, one 120 years old, with tiny garden
where lupins, fuchsias and wild roses grow. These a
rented out to holiday-makers, mainly from East and We
Falkland.

The Island Owner and Farmer

Rob McGill, 46, is a third-generation Islander – one grandfather came from Scotland, the other from Somerset. His father was a shepherd and later farm manager on Weddell Island, which was where Rob grew up. At 14 he began working as a shepherd, and in 1967 he married Lorraine. Together they bought Sea Lion Island and lived there for seven years looking after 1,700 sheep with Falkland Islands Government Beaver sea plane, able to land on a small pond, for transport. Rob and Lorraine bought Carcass Island in 1974 and are its only inhabitants. Lorraine is deputy head of the boarding hostel in Stanley for schoolchildren from Camp, and works there during term time. They have two children.

The busiest month in the year is November, and I suppose on a typical day I get up about four o'clock, have some tea or coffee and then go out and milk the cows. By six o'clock, I'll have separated the milk from the cream and started shearing the sheep and rolling the wool. Breakfast is about eight o'clock – eggs and bacon, fried bread or toast, cornflakes, bread and marmalade. I wash the dishes, go and part the cows from calves and at nine o'clock I'll be heading back to the shearing shed. I take a flask with me and have a cup of coffee there and shear a few more sheep until twelve o'clock, when I come home and have a cup of soup. I do shearing until about three o'clock, when I have a cup of tea and think, What am I going to eat this evening? By 5.30 I'll have pressed one or two bales of wool and then I come home and cook my supper. Afterwards I'll possibly disappear to the garden and do a bit of work there for an hour or so. We grow potatoes, carrots, parsley, beetroot, Brussel sprouts, yellow and white turnips, cauliflower, swedes and radishes. Then I'll have a bath and that's the end of a November day.

It takes me about fifteen days to bring the sheep in, shear them, press the wool and take it over to the jetty, but I enjoy doing it by myself and I never have time to be lonely.

I try and get the shearing out of the way before I start taking visitors into the cottages [see p.114] and before beginning baking biscuits and cakes with Aunt Agnes [who comes from Stanley to help in the summer season] for the tourist ships that stop off here on their way to the Antarctic. We started having them in 1978 and the shipping companies pay us $10 a head. The average number landing at one time is about a hundred and we have to answer a lot of questions when they're drinking their tea in the kitchen, but I enjoy having them here and have made many good friends around the world as a result. This year we'll probably make about 20,000 pieces of confectionery for ten ships, and of course we make our own butter and have full-cream milk for tea. The skimmed milk just goes into the compost heap or down the drain.

Bread is a necessity of life and I had to learn to make it after Lorraine and the children went to live in Stanley. She had always done it, so one didn't think too much about it, then suddenly she wasn't here and I didn't have any bread left. I had a look at how other people did it in a book, and

it's never been any problem to make. I cut my own hai:
too. If you can trim a hedge, you can cut hair.

We have two cottages to let and we supply visitors witl
milk and meat and fresh vegetables. We also have a grocer
store here, so people can buy from that, and supplies com*
in every few months by ship on the *Monsunen* or th*
Forrest.

In the winter I sometimes go to live in Stanley, and i*
the wool-collecting season I work as a seaman on a woc
ship, which gives me a good look round the country a*
well. I enjoy this kind of thing and think it's good to wor'
for someone else now and then, because it makes you thin'
there is a time to turn to and a time to knock off. In m
case, when I'm on my own, the time to knock off come*
much later.

I think the biggest problem in the Falklands for a paren*
is education. although the system has made great stride*
since my days of going to school. Then I might see
travelling teacher once or twice a year, because he had s*
many places to visit and had to do all his travelling by bo*
and on horseback. It's greatly improved today with rad*
lessons for younger children, but I still feel that the chil*
who is educated in Stanley in the classroom has a muc
better grasp of a situation than the one who gets rad*
lessons and a little bit of teaching from mother or fathe:
We were fortunate because Lorraine had been a Stanle
child and gone to a classroom every day, so she had a muc
better grounding than I had as a Camp-based child, an*
that's where I make my comparison. If you're going to pl*
an equal part in society, you can't just sit out in the sticl
and still expect to be able to do so.

I suppose you hope, if you train young people, you wi*
get a percentage come back. But if they go somewhere el*
in the world then at least you've done something f*
someone. Unless we can have equal pay here for equ*
qualifications for locals and expats, a greater percentage *
our trained people will go where they can earn an equ*
salary. I'd say our administration needs to app*
themselves to this or else it's partly defeating the object
the training. When the post of Chief Pilot was advertis*
recently, it was for something like £32,000, but our loc
pilots were working for £11,500 plus £2,000 for sev*
days' flying through the summer season.

As I see it, some people think the Falklands can wag the world, but I feel in the not-too-distant future we will have to try and think a bit more positively towards finding a way forward rather than staying in this constant stalemate with Argentina, for no one should ever bring armed conflict back into this area. Britain and Argentina have had a relationship for over 150 years, and to fight a war over the Falklands is absolutely disastrous. And how long can Britain afford to keep its present deterrent force in the Islands? The only situation I can think of is that if Argentina's objection is to Britain being a colonial power then we must have self-government.

If I had one wish, it would be that everyone who wanted to be in the Falklands *could* be and that those who didn't, could go home. It's not my fault that soldiers are stationed here but when I ask those who come to Carcass Island, 90% of them just hate being here. When I ask them what the problem is, they say there are no discos, no bars and no women.

But even if they wanted to come out to Camp, there's a limited number that can be transported by helicopter and a limited number of places to go to. I can also see a time when the Lodges are going to be catering more for tourists than the average soldier, and with the prices they're charging, there's a limit to what he [the soldier] can afford. If they come and camp here, farmers will be worried about fire. So there are many twists and turns to life in the Falklands, whether you are a soldier or civilian.

West Point Island

West Point Island lies off the north-west tip of West
Falkland. It is 3 miles long by 1½ miles wide and its only
inhabitants are Roddy and Lilly Napier, who run a sheep
farm, and their granddaughter Poppy, aged 7. There is
only a small airstrip, and access to the island is difficult
but it is one of the most beautiful in the Falklands, with
rookeries of rockhopper penguins and black-browed
albatrosses. Trees grow in the Napiers' garden, with roses,
lupins, foxgloves, daisies, pinks, and red-hot pokers.
Flourishing here, too, is the tiny pink Felton plant, named
after Roddy's great-uncle, who discovered it.

The Island Owners and Farmers

Roddy Napier, 60, is a third-generation Islander whose great-uncle, Arthur Felton, was the first person to settle on West Point in 1879. His wife, Lilly, 62, a fourth-generation Islander, was brought up on Carcass Island. Their daughter married an English Marine, and Roddy and Lilly adopted her child Poppy, 7, when she was fourteen months old. Now they are the only inhabitants of West Point Island. They have 1,800 sheep, and welcome visitors in the summer months.

RODDY: I've been to the Argentine many times and the war was something I'd been expecting every day for a long time. They said they'd do it in spite of what the British Government said, and they did it at more or less the time they'd warned us they would. If there had been a lease-back in the seventies, it could have been all right, there was a calmer atmosphere then. That's my opinion but most people don't think so. Lilly doesn't think so either and it's too late now.

LILLY: There's an island in the Baltic where they have three flags flying. It was Swedish and claimed by Finland, and that seems to work but they're a different race of people. We've been to the Argentine more times than I've got toes and fingers, and they're nice enough people, but not to run the country.

RODDY: Some Councillors have said we never got anything from them, but they supplied all the gas, flour and kerosene. I don't say we can't do without these things, but it's a mistake to say we never had them.

LILLY: If the Argentines had carried on as they were, they could have had the place. They used to bring in their young servicemen and the girls married them. They could have brought in some lovely girls and the boys here would have married *them*. Our daughter had Argentine boyfriends.

RODDY: We want peace but here we are ten years on and we still haven't got it. I know it's very difficult and people wouldn't like to see the Argentine planes coming in, running a service again, but I think it's inevitable, though I can't see the British Government tolerating that situation. But people in London were bombed nearly every night for four years and within weeks British soldiers were marrying German girls. It puzzles me really, but I think it's because we're an island and were so untouched before.

I think 80% of people in Camp would say they'd rather money was spent on roads than the new telephone system. Councillors were all for that but ordinary people liked the two-metre radio. They would call up Councillors, knowing others could listen to what they were saying. Now, of course, you talk to Councillors on the phone and no one else hears what they're saying, which is far less embarrassing for them. Councillors are evasive and it did put them on the spot.

LILLY: If we had a nice road here we wouldn't have to spend money on such expensive Land Rovers that cost £14,000. We could have a car.

RODDY: In the old days, sea transport was better than it is today, much more frequent. It wasn't many weeks passed when there wasn't a schooner here from Stanley Today the *Monsunen* and the *Forrest* only come once every two months. Cruise ships began coming here in 1968 and they're another source of income for us and we give them tea and show them round the garden.

LILLY: Just after the war, helicopters used to bring servicemen in for a rest but that has quietened down now I enjoyed it. It was nice to do something for them after what they'd done for us. It was a little thank you and we never charged them. Some were survivors from ships that were sunk.

RODDY: I think it's a great mistake to have this division between Camp and Stanley – I suppose it's jealousy in way. People in Camp say, 'Why should those living in Stanley have roads and television when we haven't got any?' Life is a lot easier in Stanley but the administration could make things easier than they do for people in Camp like subsidising inter-island air fares.

Life has changed in Stanley much more than in the Camp There seem to be so many rules and regulations there now Once upon a time, before '82, you knew everyone and if stranger came, people said, 'Oh, I wonder who that is?' Now you see more people you don't know than you do.

POPPY: In the morning I go out to play with Lassie and Kay, my two dogs. I smack them on the head when they do wrong so they know what not to do. Today I went up on th paddock hill and saw a baby penguin. I bow to th mollymawks [albatrosses] but they don't know what tha means. The best things are going for walks and bringing th sheep in, and last night I rode on top of their backs. A long time ago I found a little lamb that didn't have its mother, s I fed it with cow's milk. I give the chickens corn, smashed up cooked eggs, lettuce and potato peel. I can cook brea and I've made a raspberry cake for my nan. When I have school on the radio, I do numbers and my diary, and m teacher gives me figures for doing good work.

North Arm Farm Settlement

This settlement lies in the south-east of East Falkland and was owned by the Falkland Islands Company before being sold to the Falkland Islands' Government in 1991. It covers 276,741 acres, and is 90 miles and four and a half hours' drive from Stanley. Thirty-five people live here; there's one store, a school and a community centre used for whist drives, dances, darts matches and two-nighters [see p.32].

The Farm Manager

Eric Goss, 50, whose family has lived in the Falklands since the 1850s, first came to North Arm when he was 17 in 1958. He worked as a shepherd, as a seaman on the coastal steamer RMS Darwin, *and in the building trade before joining the Falkland Islands Company in 1971 as an assistant manager. Eric is married to Shirley, a fifth-generation Islander, and they have two sons: William, who represented the Falklands in the Commonwealth Games in New Zealand in 1990, and Morgan, an engineer with the Falkland Islands Government Air Service. They own eighteen horses, including an Arab stallion. As a jockey, Eric has won fifty-eight silver trophies.*

At eighteen I was living very happily in an isolated shepherd's house 12 miles from North Arm until the manager thought it was wrong to have a young fellow there on his own, working with unruly horses, and only an intermittent land-line telephone system. My mother had learnt me to cook bread and cake, and there's no better pupil in cooking than a hungry lad. I had Tilley lamps for light, and an old windcharger with a 6-volt battery, and a GEC radio that gave me the London news about every second night. I'd take flour, seasoning, jams and sauces from the settlement, and you killed your own sheep for mutton. A shepherd's house didn't have a garden, so you lived out of the tin if you wanted vegetables.

I never felt lonely – as long as you're on your own how can you be? The only problems in the world are caused by people, and if you haven't got any around you, there's no one to argue with.

Now I start my day at five in the morning, make up the talley boards [the records of the shearing], come home for breakfast, go back to the shearing shed about a mile away by nine o'clock, come home briefly for lunch and finish my day outside at six o'clock. Then I have an hour's work in the office putting all the records into a ledger, so if I hop a twig during the night they're here for someone to pick up the tabs.

At Port Howard they advertise for shepherds who can ride motorbikes, but I think they're cowboys. They use revolvers and make a lot of noise and frighten the sheep and one of these days they're going to shoot a shepherd that's for sure. The bikes go too quick for the dogs and too quick for the sheep, so half of them stay in the camp. Whenever I put my shepherds on motorbikes – I've got a couple but they're mostly in the garage wrecked – I find it frightfully expensive and very frustrating trying to keep the machinery going, for they're not skilled machine operators, and the bike rivets the spine of a man so he's bit of a zombie after a time. I don't believe they're the answer for gathering sheep in large tracts of land, whereas the horse, the dog and sheep are all compatible in moving across it.

I became a Councillor because other people asked me to There's only a few of us who will stand up and have a g in a small community like this. There was a lot of hass and badgering. 'Come on, you can do it. The Governor wants another Councillor.' Finally, there were four others standing, but I won the seat with flying colours, though I was beaten in this last election. I was nobody's puppet but I was in touch with my constituents, and my main baseline was what I knew was right for the Falklands. I could never follow a party line because this might conflict with what I believed, and I really like the present individuality of government. I was on the Council three years and kept the duty on cigarettes down for two of them until I conceded on that because I was convinced it was a definite health hazard. I won a freezing of tax increases for three years and if any of the new Councillors can achieve as much as I did in that line I'll be very pleased with them.

Some good things have come out of the Conflict – we were stagnating before that, there's no doubt about it. In 1978 Ted Rowlands, then Minister of State, came to Goose Green where I was manager, and I tried to persuade him to set up fishing boundaries and get some revenue, as the Japanese, Polish and Russians were just hoovering up the fish and there was no control and no revenue. But Ted Rowlands put his arm round my shoulder and led me away from all the reporters and said, 'Let's just go quietly and talk this out. We'll arrive at it one day, but this is not the time to talk about it.'

The invasion brought us into the focus of the world and now we've moved into a faster ball game, a different way of life. We're catching up on the rat race that takes place in Britain and all developed countries, and with this come the stresses and strains that take a heavy toll on the human race, and contentment disappears.

Sea Lion Island

Sea Lion, 4 miles by one, is the most southerly and isolated of the inhabited islands, with nothing between it and the Antarctic some 1,000 miles away. Until government float-planes were introduced in the early 1950s, ships only visited the island once or twice a year to pick up wool and leave mail and provisions. Now boats call three or four times a year and the cargo is winched up a steep cliff. Aircraft bring in visitors most days in the summer.

Until a Tourist Lodge was built here in 1986, farmers Terry and Doreen Clifton were the island's only inhabitants. Now the Lodge, which has five twin bedrooms all with en suite shower and toilets and is owned by the Falkland Islands Development Corporation, attracts tourists all through the summer months. They come to see the thousands of penguins and elephant seals, and the many different species of birds, including the striated caracara, one of the rarest birds of prey in the world.

In 1990 the Cliftons, who planted 60,000 tussac-grass plants here, sold the island to the Falkland Islands Development Corporation. It may now be used as a wildlife study centre.

On the southern cliffs of the island is a memorial to the men who died on *HMS Sheffield* in the 1982 war.

The Tourist-Lodge Managers

In 1974 David and Pat Gray sold their house in Middlesbrough and moved with their 3-year-old daughter to the Falklands for the freedom it offered. David worked as an electrician at Goose Green and Pat learnt to make her own bread, milk a cow and cook with peat. After twelve years they moved to Sea Lion Island, owned and inhabited only by Terry and Doreen Clifton and their two children, to run a newly built Tourist Lodge. The Grays now have two daughters: Andrea, who is at university, and Johan, 15, at school in Stanley.

DAVID: People come from all over the world to see the wildlife here, and Japanese and Korean fishing companies hold seminars in the Lodge. We also have scientists, botanists and marine biologists. I take people on tours of the island and have to be aware of what they're all doing, because they may step on an elephant seal, or not see a sea lion lurking there.

The Lodge is going well but we do have the problem of how many people do we want in a place like this? We don't want crowds because that would upset the wildlife, so we have to try and get a balance between being businesslike and also wildlife conservationists. We do get some people, one photographer for instance, who disturbed nesting penguins – it was anything for a shot – and if I find someone doing something like that now I just put him straight on a plane back to Stanley. If we don't protect the wildlife, there's nothing for anyone to come here for and anyway the place doesn't belong to us, it's just on loan and we should give it back as we got it, not destroy it for future generations.

The best time to come? September is good for elephant seals, the big males are planning out their beach areas, the females coming ashore, the first pups being born; jackass penguins are arriving and digging out their holes. It's an ideal time for trout fishing too. In the following months the gentoo penguins are starting their nests, king penguins will be there and all the small birds nesting. End of October, November, you have the return of rockhopper and macaroni penguins, and the seabirds start to arrive. The sea lions are here all the year round, but more come ashore at the end of December and January, and they have their pups, mating in colonies. In January the gentoo and jackass chicks are all learning about life, going to sea. In February, the female sea lions start drifting away with their pups, the big bulls roaming up and down the beach. Things quieten down in March but all this time, in the sea, the beaches are patrolled by killer whales and in December, January and February there are sightings of blue whales and dolphins. There's something every moment of the year but one of the best things we have here is peace and quiet. I mean real, genuine peace and quiet.

We grow all our own vegetables and are almost self-sufficient. We use peat for heating and cooking, but it's very labour-intensive and we've thought of switching to diesel because you have more control. There's only three of us here to run the Lodge and with more and more guests we just haven't got the time to put in the peat every hour.

Johan is at school in Stanley and she does miss being at home. Last year she was swimming with the sea lions and playing with the elephant pups in the water. If we had our time again, we'd never send our children away. We only see them for six weeks in the summer, one at Christmas, two at Easter. We really need better education in Camp so they don't have to go away to Stanley, but how we're going to get it no one knows.

PAT: It's a full day from 7.30 in the morning to 10.30 at night. I try and catch an hour or two in the afternoon when people have gone out, otherwise I think I'd keel over. We do push ourselves along but I enjoy what I'm doing. We're in control, no one interferes, and that's what we like. I don't regret coming out here but I miss silly things like getting my hair done regularly. When we go home, which we do every three years, I do like to go shopping, but in fact I've got used to doing it once a year with a UK catalogue.

JOHAN: You usually go into Stanley to school when you're ten and until then you have to talk to teachers on the radio and get a Camp teacher every few months. Some of the children like keeping to themselves, but you can just pitch in with them. I was very shy at the beginning myself. Now it's all right and I can talk to anyone. When I first went to school in Stanley I was really homesick, I was crying to come home, but I'm used to it now and it doesn't bother me at all, and I'm glad to get back there sometimes. When you're out here you have nothing to do once you've seen everything once or twice. But I hated being away from Mum and Dad at first, and I say now I don't want to go to college because it's so far away. I want to work with animals in the wild where there are trees. There aren't any here.

I never want to go back to the UK. I don't like it. It's too crowded. I like being out here because it's fresh, if you get my meaning. I keep saying to Dad I don't like being in the UK because it's polluted – I watch a lot of documentaries about pollution in the UK and it scares me to think it's killing all the animals.

In the holidays I help Mum do the rooms, and I used to milk the cow for Doreen and Terry Clifton when they were away, and looked after their four dogs and fed the hens. I go out on my bike, which I started driving two years ago – you don't have to have a crash helmet because if you fall the grass is soft. Or I stay here and read books and write letters. I like videos more than TV because with TV you have to watch what's on or not at all. With video you can pick what you want.

Some of my friends come here and don't like it. They criticise us Islanders and call us Bennies [see p.78] and think it's really boring. It's just the way they are, I suppose.

One thing that will never go out of my mind and that's the war. We were at Goose Green and I was five. Mum keeps telling me that Andrea started crying and that I slept quite a way through it but I remember we weren't given very much to eat except cold beans. When the stores came in, we got pillows and cereal but it was very difficult staying in one room. You had to be friendly with people and not get angry with them, just had to make do, and we read books and played games. To me, the Argies were like strangers from another place, coming down and taking us and putting us in the hall [the community centre], and I was wondering why they were doing this. There was one person who tried to make radio contact and got caught and was taken away and tied up. Our home, when we got back to it, was in a right mess, and the Argies had eaten all our food.

The thing that I don't like is that UK people come down and want to change everything. I think that's wrong, but I suppose we just have to put up with it.

Mount Pleasant

It took 3,000 people just eighty weeks to build the Mount Pleasant complex, consisting of a small town, a military base and an airfield, on isolated, virgin territory in East Falkland. At the same time, they were constructing a 35-mile road through minefields to link this with Stanley. The project cost £600 million and the British Government now pay £64 million a year for the total defence of the Falklands.

Two thousand servicemen from three services (60% air force, 30% army, 10% navy), together with some civilians, live here, and a commander – a Rear Admiral, Major General or Air-Vice Marshal – comes down to take over for a year at a time. A small number of married officers and civilians, on a twelve-month tour, live in bungalows, but most of the service personnel, on unaccompanied four-month tours of duty, live in a sprawling building which is linked by a 2-kilometre-long covered 'street' leading to dining rooms, NAAFI services, shops and an interdenominational church. There are sports facilities, clubs, a cinema and video room, a hairdressing salon, bars, a film-processing and printing business, and a small library. A water-sports centre has been established on a lake between Mount Pleasant and Mare Harbour, with canoes, kayaks, dinghies and facilities for water skiing and windsurfing.

Military transport to Stanley is by a 4-tonne lorry which takes about an hour each way. A regular bus service runs seven days a week from the Domestic Complex to Mare Harbour and around the airfield. Six Land Rovers can be hired for personal use at £10 a day and 10p a mile, and servicemen are encouraged, in their free time, to explore the countryside and see the spectacular wildlife of the Falklands.

A booklet entitled *Welcome to the Falklands* is published for those at the base, and apart from giving a potted history of the Falklands and describing the work of the servicemen stationed there, it provides an invaluable list of the initials which military personnel and Falkland Islanders use for just about everything.

The Military
Commander

*Major General Paul
Stevenson, 50, was in
command of British Forces
Falkland Islands from 1989 to
1990.*

I think it would have been better to have the base nearer Stanley, but the reason I suspect it was built here was that it was cheaper and more efficient to start with a green-field site rather than try and develop Stanley airfield itself. But we do sit on our own as a totally self-contained town and it is different from other garrisons. It's 8,000 miles from home and the one outlet is through the Tristar air-bridge, so you can't go anywhere off the Islands. It's quite difficult to go anywhere *on* the Islands because apart from Camp tracks, which are passable in summer but not for much of the winter, there aren't any roads except for the one to Stanley. So you've got to go around by helicopter, which means booking in advance. And there is very little off-base entertainment, no taxis outside the gate, no girls, no pubs half a mile away, so everything actually conspires against getting people off the base and mixing with the local community.

Having a civil/military liaison hat, I sit on the Executive and Legislative Councils as the Governor's defence adviser, and know a lot about what goes on in the Falkland Islands' Government. But in order to put that into context and make it mean something, my wife and I spend quite a lot of time going round the farm settlements – about once a week if I can.

I think people welcome it and are reassured that we're here. In England you would get an outcry if a Phantom flew over at a hideously low height, but here, people think it's good news. The big difficulty is enthusing those on the base to actually get out into Camp, especially in winter. But when they do go, they always enjoy it, and the Phantom pilots have adopted a farm and get a couple of days there.

My wife has been involved in running a project to find work for wives on the base. There are three shops in the complex now, almost totally manned by the wives, which provide a very valuable facility for the men. There is a Stanley Wives group and they come out here for social functions and a monthly lunch.

I don't think there's anything that will change the men's attitude to being down here and the fact that they greet each incoming plane with a cluster of posters – the Gozomi charts – stating the number of days they have before going home. But the great thing is to keep people's spirits and morale up while they are here. They obviously don't like being separated from their wives and we'd like to have more [wives] coming down for a short term, but there's no money in the programme to build more married quarters. A lot of men when they get down here say, 'If I'd known what it was like before I left England, I'd have wanted to spend longer and bring my wife.' It's because it's had such a bad press. What we're trying to do now is negate that and talk more about the good points. I think everyone here finds the work professionally rewarding, and on the social side each wing runs its own bar and club. There are aerobics and weight-training sessions and the eight squash courts are booked up three days ahead.

As I said, I'd like to see more people going out into Camp not only because it's better for us but because it's putting some money into the local economy. One of the ongoing issues is about buying food produced locally for the base. At the moment we have a major project running to try and persuade local people to give us food in sufficient quantity to the standard we need, and to guarantee it, because then we would buy it from them. But at the moment, a cow is being killed in Montevideo, shipped to England and then brought back down here. I do want to buy stuff locally but they've got to provide the service.

The Young Mother

Tracy Jones, 28, a former naval nurse, comes from Norfolk. Her husband Richard is Radio Station Manager at Mount Pleasant, and before coming to the Falklands they worked in Gibraltar and Germany.

Most of the day is taken up with looking after Ashley, who is six months old, because there are not the facilities like a toddlers' group that you would normally find at home. It's difficult with things like baby food, and we have to get a tuck box from Granny [in the UK] every now and again. The same with nappies. They do have a few in Stanley but it really depends on when the ship is next due, as they do tend to run out.

Being here is a bit like the *Marie Celeste* because all the other wives have jobs, and having a baby – Ashley is the only one – does restrict your life. It's lonely sometimes but there are always people to talk to and you can have a coffee in The Oasis [café], which really *is* like an oasis in the desert. We go for walks and you certainly get a nice fresh breeze – once we were walking along a corridor and came out into an open part, and a great gust of wind took the pram about a foot off the ground.

We arrived in time for the good weather. But you have to be careful even when you think it's going to be fine, because I can put the baby out in beautiful sunshine and half an hour later I see clouds coming over and you suddenly get hail. It's very variable. You get the impression from the media that the Falklands are very wild, but they're really quite beautiful and you certainly get to learn how our grandparents had to cope without the mod cons of modern living.

I think more people with young children are being encouraged to come down here and I'd like to start up a crèche or some facility like that. There's a very good school here and anyone with a school-aged child can get a part-time job. There are seven children at the moment, with another three coming at the end of the month.

I think what I miss most is fresh milk and sometimes I think I would kill for a glass of it! We could get it from Camp but Ashley would need a BCG injection to avoid the possibility of TB. You can get pasties at the NAAFI, which are a great favourite, and things like fish fingers, but you can't get all the food we take for granted at home, like pâté, for instance. If the ship is going to be late, we don't get any fruit either because it gets off-loaded at Ascension Island.

It's very much a separate world here, but among the boys the camaraderie with us civilians is very good. If we're walking along the corridor, we're invariably invited in for a coffee and the soldiers all take turns in holding the baby. Many of them say, 'Let's have a cuddle because we haven't seen a baby for four months.' Or, 'My baby was just about this size the last time I saw him.' It's nice for them and it's also good for us, and we have no problems at all getting baby-sitters! I advertise by adding 'supper available', which is something they all like, and if you also put 'bath available' and 'home comforts' (a real settee and things like that) you get masses of replies.

The Photographic Technician

Norman Clark, BEM was a Royal Marine for twenty-two years, some of which were spent in the Falklands. He left the Service in 1983 and became one of sixteen ex-servicemen to return to live in the Islands. In 1989 he opened a mini-lab to process and print films at Mount Pleasant, and now runs Falkland Printz Ltd. He is 48 years old and married to June, who works with him in the company.

We live in Stanley and travel up that dusty road to Mount Pleasant every day. I think we know all the potholes personally. It's only 35 miles long but in the middle of winter, with two punctures and no more spare tyres, it might as well be 300 miles away. But I don't mind that. The M1 in the UK can be boring but life on the MPA [Mount Pleasant Airport] road is different every day and if you do break down, no local person will ever pass you by – they'll stop and help you or go and get someone who can. People care about people here and we can let our kids go out to play for as long as they like, without any fear of them being abducted.

You have to learn to sort out a lot of things for yourself. For instance, when you get somebody down from the UK to install something and they go back four days later, you can have problems. There's a great urge to pick up the phone and say 'Help!' but you have to say to yourself, Well, hang on a minute, read this one through and work it out yourself. Which is, in fact, what the Falklands are all about.

We opened this shop in December 1989 and for two days had a continuous queue of people handing in piles of films. I think we took something like 2,000 in that time, which gave us an instant backlog. I was a photographer in the Marines for about ten years or so, so I was no stranger to that, but the actual volume of stuff that was put through did floor me for a while. At the beginning, Kodak said to me sceptically there was no way we could do 3,000 films a month, but we do.

And you've got this other myth which is called the Falklands Factor. Well, there isn't one actually. The factor is at the other end of the Atlantic and it's British companies forgetting to get cargo to ships on time, and vehicles not turning up at warehouses when they are supposed to. That's the true Falklands Factor.

I've become very involved in setting up the '82 Trust, which will provide holidays for members and former members of the Services. The idea is for servicemen to revisit their place of trauma, shall we call it, and then stay with a Falklands family for the summer and see other aspects of the Islands which they wouldn't have seen in 1982. When some families came down to the Falklands recently they might have thought on arrival that the place wasn't worth their son's life. But by the time they went back ten days later they were totally converted. If that sort of feeling is put over amongst those who actually grieved for their sons or husbands, then I think the same thing could apply to guys who have not been able to keep a job down because of what they experienced here in the war. The therapy is coming back and seeing the Islands in a different light.

The Squadron Leader

Robin Singleton joined the air force in 1961 straight from school. She now works in administration at Mount Pleasant Military Base. Married for twenty years, Robin came to the Falklands with her husband, a serving officer, in 1989, when they were the first couple both in the Services to be stationed on the Islands.

I'd like to get into Camp more often but as there are no roads away from the Stanley area, you have to go by air, and military aircraft are very limited. We've been to Pebble Island and Port Howard and have driven over to Goose Green, but although it's only 19 miles away it can take anything up to two hours to get there. If you're inexperienced drivers, you need to go in two vehicles, because if one gets bogged down the other one can pull you out.

I think there are a lot of misconceptions about the Falklands. People said to me before I came, 'Why go there, it's the back of beyond?' and there's the standard joke of, 'It's not the end of the world, but you can see it from there.' In fact, its climate is no worse than many places in the UK, but what is different is the strong wind that blows virtually all the time. The wildlife is absolutely fantastic and the air is so clear you can see for miles and miles.

I think I'll be quite sorry to go because my life here has a quiet, gentle pace. There's no mad rush to achieve everything yesterday.

The Mission Worker

Sally Clarke, a 53-year-old widow from Belfast, came to the Falklands on a two-year contract with the Mission to Military Garrisons after spending six months in Cyprus. She is one of three members running the alcohol-free Oasis Club at the base.

The Oasis was started by some Christians down here whc saw a need for a place where the lads could go apart from the bars. I mean, you don't always want to be in the ba: every night, do you? It's a quiet and peaceful room here and doesn't feel, I hope, as if you were in the middle of a military base. We have newspapers that come in twice a week on the plane from Britain, there are games the lads can play and they can write their blueys [airmail letters] We're open from 2 pm to 4.30 pm, and 6 to 10 pm, sever days a week, and provide soft drinks and bake our own cakes and pastries, gingerbreads and fruit loaves.

On Monday and Friday evenings we have Bible study and a discussion group on Wednesday evenings. There' another quiet room, too, where they can come with problems but they also like to share good news as well They get the feeling here that someone cares, you know that someone's interested in them. And of course, the Padre is always on call. We work very much hand in hand with him.

The Boutique Manager

Penny Phillips, a colonel's wife, is manager of the Gozomi Boutique.

Before I arrived I thought the Falklands were barren wasteland where I would get one tomato a year if I wa lucky. I came with thermal underwear coming out of m ears and, of course, here I am covered in sunburn an wearing a summer dress.

Index

THE FALKLAND ISLANDS

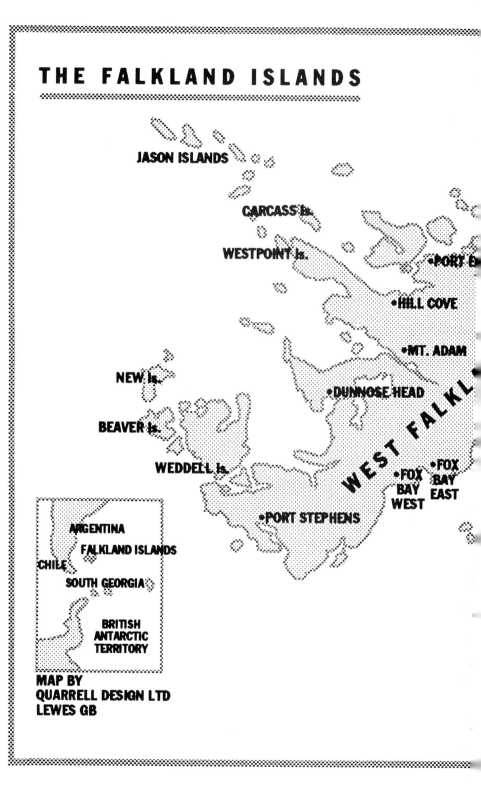

JASON ISLANDS

CARCASS Is.

WESTPOINT Is.

•PORT E

•HILL COVE

•MT. ADAM

NEW Is.

•DUNNOSE HEAD

BEAVER Is.

WEDDELL Is.

WEST FALKL

•FOX
BAY
EAST

•FOX
BAY
WEST

•PORT STEPHENS

ARGENTINA

FALKLAND ISLANDS

CHILE

SOUTH GEORGIA

BRITISH
ANTARCTIC
TERRITORY

MAP BY
QUARRELL DESIGN LTD
LEWES GB